lighting
styles

First published in 1999 by Hamlyn an imprint of Octopus
Publishing Group Limited, 2-4 Heron Quays, London E14 4JP

© Octopus Publishing Group Limited 1999

Distributed in the United States by Sterling Publishing Co., Inc.
387 Park Avenue South, New York, NY 10016-8810

Publishing Director Laura Bamford
Executive Editor Mike Evans
Senior Editor Nina Sharman
Editor Michelle Pickering

Creative Director Keith Martin
Executive Art Editor Geoff Borin
Designer Mike Moule

Picture Research Joanne Beardwell
Production Controller Phillip Chamberlain

A catalogue record for this book is available from the
British Library

hardback ISBN 0 600 59763 6
paperback ISBN 0 600 60093 9

The publishers have made every effort to ensure that all
instructions given in this book are accurate and safe, but the
cannot accept liability for any resulting injury, damage or los
either person or property whether direct or consequential a
howsoever arising. The author and publishers will be grate
any information which will assist them in keeping future
up to date.

Produced by Toppan Printing Co Ltd

Printed in China

lighting styles

siân rees

styles

hamlyn

introduction 6

what is light? 8

hallways 18 | living rooms 26 | kitchens 40 | dining rooms 5

contents

bedrooms 66

studies 80

bathrooms 88

gardens 102

practicalities 114

directory of suppliers 124

index 126

acknowledgments 128

introduction

Lighting the rooms of your home is not just about illumination. It is about creating a mood, expressing yourself, taking pleasure in your surroundings, feeling relaxed and happy in your home. In simple terms, it's about the feel-good factor.

These are exciting times. New technology is pushing back the boundaries to make high-tech light sources readily available in the domestic arena. This, coupled with an increasing awareness of the effects of lighting in the home and the myriad lighting design possibilities, has meant that contemporary lighting styles have improved dramatically in recent years.

So many new developments have occurred that the standard tungsten bulb might appear to be the dinosaur of the lighting world. In fact, it still has a lot to offer, not least the warm, relaxing quality of its illumination. In addition, lighting designers are radically updating all areas of fittings, so we can look forward to chic new ways of enjoying this traditional form of lighting as well as the new styles of low-voltage halogen.

There is no doubt that the advent of halogen, and in particular low-voltage halogen, has been largely responsible for the latest wave of state-of-the-art lights, some of them almost sculptural in their appeal. Not only does halogen emit a far crisper, bright white light than tungsten, but the new bulbs are also extremely small. This compact size has given designers great scope for furthering their minimalist, space-age inventions.

The low-voltage factor has in itself sparked a revolution. Because the 12-volt current can be safely carried in unprotected wires, and even touched without injury, so-called "bare-wire" installations have become the latest vogue. The halogen capsules or dichroic reflectors are suspended on the wires and can be freely moved to wherever they are required. This has led to the development of ultra high-tech lighting effects for modern interiors, with the wires stretched tautly from wall to wall or even vertically between the floor and ceiling. Such flexible lighting is not only simple and elegant, it also offers the perfect solution for the large, open-plan living spaces of today's converted warehouses and loft apartments.

It is not just modern homes that can benefit from the new developments in lighting – any room in any style of home can be given a new look by choosing one of the latest eye-catching, innovative lamps. Designers are exploring every possible material, from quirky origami-style plastics and sleek metallic foil to images of outer space with sputnik-style paper globes on tiny tripod feet.

Pendants have undergone a complete transformation, too, and re-emerged with far greater style than could ever have been imagined when looking back on their forerunners. Giant, industrial aluminium shades for the kitchen are reminiscent of the utilitarianism of the factory floor and are an inspired choice for the latest, catering-style work areas. Elsewhere, particularly in dining rooms, compact glass pendants hanging together in staggered groups represent nothing less than visual artistry.

Fluorescent lighting has also seen great advances. Once the poor relation of lighting with little to recommend it except economy, the current generation of compact fluorescents give a warmer, less pallid light than before and have been repackaged in wittily shaped tubes that can be curved around mirrors for both a practical and aesthetic approach to bathroom lighting.

In this book we look at how to harness all these advances in order to create the ultimate lighting effect for every room in the home. Selecting fittings can be thoroughly bewildering, particularly now that the choice is so great, so here we show you what is possible and explain how to achieve the look. It is no longer just a question of deciding on the style of the fitting – you need to think about the quality of the illumination it will produce, where it should be positioned for best effect and how it will interact with other lamps in your scheme. Nothing should be considered in isolation.

Don't feel overwhelmed. Many people mistakenly think that lighting is a complex subject full of confusing jargon and technical wizardry. In fact, once you have understood the basic lighting options available, you will be inspired by the infinite possibilities open to you, at the flick of a switch. And that is when the real fun begins. Enjoy!

▶ Glass bricks have been used here to "borrow" light from an adjacent room. The floor-lamp throws the light up and away creating an attractive, diffuse ambient light.

what is light ?

There is no mistaking the golden rule of interior design: good lighting is the single most important factor in decorating your home – without it, the other elements, such as colour, shape and form, would simply be invisible.

Lighting a room is an exciting task. Good lighting can make an otherwise ordinary room feel special. You can impose a dramatic change on your environment by changing a single light bulb, so think what a whole new lighting scheme could do.

Before you choose your light fittings, you need to consider a few fundamental questions. Ask yourself what sort of lighting you want – intense, soft, bright or moody? Where do you want the light – in the corners, over your work area, at eye level, coming from the ceiling or at shoulder height? Do the light fittings need to be movable or can they be fixed in position? What sort of feeling are you trying to create – relaxing, invigorating or convivial?

Translating your lighting requirements into tangible fittings and sockets begins to sound like a daunting task! However, a lighting scheme is actually quite easy to plan if you consider everything in terms of the four basic types of lighting. Every variation you can think of will fit into one of these categories and, having determined the category you require, you can go on to choose your individual fittings. Briefly, the four lighting categories are as follows:

Ambient lighting: This is the name given to the light all around us, the general background illumination. The most basic form of ambient lighting is daylight. For the home, ambient light can be supplied by one source or, far more effectively, by many.

Task lighting: This is the rather basic name given to the type of light by which an activity is carried out, be it writing at a desk, reading in bed or chopping vegetables in the kitchen.

Accent lighting: This denotes the type of lighting that is used to highlight individual features, which can be as diverse as sculptures, pictures, bookcases or plants.

Decorative lighting: This is light used primarily for decoration rather than illumination. It includes quirky lava and fibre-optic lamps, decorative neon signs, the twinkling spots of a chandelier and the kinetic (moving) light of flickering candles and firelight.

▶ The minimalist architecture of this apartment is enhanced by the incorporation of many windows and maximum daylight.

▲ Good, all-round, that is, ambient lighting is essential in the kitchen. The best quality results from multiple sources.

▲ With large windows and a sunny aspect, you may wish to reduce the level of light with shutters or Venetian blinds.

Ambient lighting

Ambient light is the light we are able to see by and surrounds us all of the time, whether it originates from the sun, moon or artificial sources. The best type of ambient light comes from an indeterminate source; just as on a grey day you cannot identify the position of the sun, the same theory should apply to ambient lighting from an artificial source – it should be glare-free, soft, shadowless and the same level of intensity all around. All of the rooms in your home will require artificial ambient lighting as a substitute for natural daylight after dark, but its characteristics will vary from room to room.

Traditionally, the most common sources of ambient light are pendant fittings and fluorescent strips. However, these can often be inappropriate, depending on the setting, and should rarely be used in isolation. Although a single pendant fitting can provide adequate ambient light to see by, the quality is poor – the pendant produces an intense pool of light immediately beneath the fitting but the level of illumination diminishes to shadowy gloom in the far corners of the room. Similarly, a fluorescent strip light will produce sufficient ambient light but the quality of the light is dubious. Fluorescent lighting contains strong peaks in the yellow/green region of the colour spectrum that give an unattractive, bilious colour to skin tones and soft furnishings.

A far better arrangement for good-quality ambient lighting is to use a number of different light sources throughout the room, so that the overall result is a diffuse, even spread of illumination. The ambient lighting can then be defined as the total output of all these different light sources. For example, a collection of lamps spread around the room may be sufficient to create a relaxing ambient

▲ A cosy, intimate atmosphere can be achieved by utilizing a pair of tungsten lamps and leaving them permanently switched on.

light in a sitting room. You may find that a series of wall washers, plus a couple of task lights, are all that is required for a bedroom. The number of fittings needed to create good ambient light is clearly proportional to the size of the room. In addition, the lights should usually be dimmable, to provide greater flexibility to your lighting scheme.

You should also consider the level of natural daylight available. If the room has large, unfettered windows and benefits from a south-facing aspect, you may not need to supplement the level of ambient light at all during the daytime. Conversely, in a basement or north-facing room with a single small window, you will have to increase the level of ambient light using electrical fittings throughout the day. Bear in mind also that northern light has a bluish

tinge, which is best countered with the incandescent, yellow light produced by a glowing tungsten filament – that is, a standard tungsten light bulb.

If you want to imitate natural daylight, there are several methods. First, look out for special "daylight" bulbs. Although these are tungsten bulbs, they have blue-coloured glass around the element to produce a cooler tone of light similar to daylight. Low-voltage halogen is also an excellent way to mimic daylight. In this type of bulb, the filament burns at a far higher temperature than ordinary tungsten, so the light is whiter and gives better colour rendering, just like natural light. It is by far the best choice for ambient lighting in a kitchen, for instance, where you need to see the colours of food accurately.

▼ Choose the right style of fitting and even a clip-on task light can look chic. Their versatility makes them perfect for work areas.

▲ Adjustable metal task lights are replacing traditional bedside lamps in many modern interiors.

Task lighting

Task lighting allows us to carry out specific activities, such as reading and writing, in a safe, efficient and comfortable environment. This usually involves lighting a fairly small and discreet area, such as a desk top or kitchen counter, the pages of a book or a sheet of music. Good task lamps should therefore be flexible, so that they can be angled and directed at exactly the right spot. As well as being mechanically flexible, good task lights may also be fitted with integral opaque reflectors that can be adjusted to redirect the light in different directions while the source – the bulb – remains unseen.

The positioning of task lights is also crucial: you should be able to adjust the direction of the light easily without the need to get up and move it. To eliminate glare, the bulb should not be visible. Glare can be very tiring to the eye and even temporarily dazzle the retina.

If you put together a collection of task lights, their output can be sufficient to create a good level of ambient light. However, in general, task lights comprise a bright, direct beam that is in contrast to the surroundings and can be tiring and uncomfortable unless used in conjunction with additional background lighting.

There are exceptions, however. In a sitting room, for example, a series of table lamps or a pair of wall downlighters placed adjacent to a sofa or chairs for reading can create a cosy, relaxed atmosphere that needs no supplementary light. Similarly, in a kitchen a number of low-voltage halogen downlighters trained on the work surface as task lights can be sufficient to light the whole room. Conversely, a couple of unobtrusive downlighters, mounted into a wall unit above the work surface, can provide an intense practical light source for detailed work while the rest of the kitchen remains in virtual darkness.

▲ Form and function go hand-in-hand in this sitting room where industrial-style task lights provide the perfect lighting solution.

Task lights are best when they are movable and adjustable – a light clipped to a shelf above a work area, for instance. If you are able to fit the task lights with dimmer controls, you will have an even more flexible lighting scheme. A pair of wall-mounted bedside lights, for example, can be bright enough to produce a good level of cosy ambient light as well as providing an effective task light to read by. When installed with separate dimmer controls, one light can turned up bright enough for one partner to read by while the remaining light is dimmed, leaving the other person dozing undisturbed.

A crown-silvered bulb can be a good choice for traditional lamp lights because it throws the light directly down onto the work surface below – the light cannot penetrate the opaque reflective coating at the top of the bulb. Remember that in a bedroom or sitting room where you wish to create a cosy, relaxed mood, any lamps should be shielded with opaque shades. In this way, the light will not be able to permeate the shade and cause glare to anyone nearby. Instead, the light is directed solely down onto the "work area" below the lamp – that is, the dressing table or pages of a book.

▲ A series of low voltage halogen uplighters and downlighters provide ambient light, whilst also highlighting a key painting.

Accent lighting

Accent lighting allows you to highlight features of interest in a room in a stylish and evocative way. They can be anything from architectural features, mouldings and bookcases to more personal items and favourite collections, such as photographs, sculptures, plants and works of art. Accent lighting is a specific, defined light directed over a fairly small area to emphasize it. While ambient lighting tends to be a bland, undefined quality of illumination that flattens out the impact of individual items in the room, accent lighting does the opposite by bringing to attention certain focuses and features of interest with intense areas of light.

The light fittings used for accent lighting can take a variety of forms, depending on the position of the item to be highlighted and its size. A collection of modern glass ornaments placed on a glass shelf can be accented by a series of low-voltage halogen down- or uplighters. Lighting the items from the side with horizontal beams of light is another option. An individual miniature looks best when lit with a discreet low-voltage halogen spotlight on a flexible arm extended in front of it.

▼ Use thick glass shelving combined with a low voltage halogen spotlight to create the perfect display case for treasured objects.

▼ Here a collection of modern vases are lit by a tungsten spotlight, recessed into the base of the glass shelf unit.

◄ A false ceiling provides a hide-away for old books, but can also conceal a light source used to throw out a narrow accent beam.

If your room has an alcove, you can draw attention to it with a single halogen downlighter set into the alcove's ceiling. Place a vase of flowers or a row of books in the alcove and the light will make it a striking feature. Accent lighting works best when combined with a simple display – an overly ornate sculpture or fussy arrangement of ornaments can look excessive if further emphasized with accent lighting.

One effect that is well worth considering, even in the most modest apartment, is highlighting the stairs. A series of low-level spotlights set into the wall beside a staircase will accent each tread to great effect. Not only does this light the way, which is useful from a safety point of view, it can also attractively highlight a natural flooring material. The striations and textures of riven slate, limestone or even rough-hewn concrete have a beauty all their own when accented by such a lighting scheme.

As with task lighting, the idea is that the area being lit – the painting or work of art, for example – becomes the focus and not the light source itself, which should be virtually invisible. An accent light that is more dazzling than the decorative feature it is supposed to highlight is not doing its job efficiently or effectively.

▲ Increasingly, light is being used as a decorative feature in its own right – particularly by architectural designers.

Accent lighting is a great way to add a sense of drama to an interior but it is easy to get carried away. If in doubt, keep accent lighting to a minimum – it is far better to exercise discretion unless you live in a house of grand proportions that can carry it off with *élan*.

Decorative lighting

While accent lighting is used to draw attention to an attractive object or feature, decorative lighting is attractive in its own right. It is designed simply to be pleasing to look at. Although decorative lighting can sometimes add to the level of ambient light in a room, this is not its prime function. Decorative lighting includes kinetic, or moving, light – the flickering flames of candles, flares and firelight.

Because it is devoid of function and devoted to aesthetics, decorative lighting has to be combined with other types of lighting to put it into a practical context. It is the icing on the cake, if you like, but no less important for that. Why shouldn't we use every available medium to intrigue our visual senses and enhance the enjoyment of our homes?

At its most simple, a decorative light can be a plain candlestick holding a single burning candle at the dining table or a string of fairy lights arranged to highlight a picture, mirror, window sill or set beneath a glass-topped table. This type of decoration is most usually associated with Christmas, but there is no reason why you cannot use the tiny, low-heat lights to adorn your home at any time. Another simple idea is to suspend a series of coloured, bare bulbs in the corner of a room, as an expression of the artistry of light.

At the other end of the scale, decorative lighting can take the form of an elaborate crystal chandelier fitted with tiny low-voltage capsules that throw twinkling splashes of light around an entrance hall but actually give out very little in the way of illumination. Decorative lights are the fun side of lighting your home, to be enjoyed once you have finalized the more practical lighting scheme, so let your imagination run wild.

Choose decorative lights that will reflect and enhance the character of your interior. The 1970s-style lava lamp is currently enjoying a revival – this kitsch decorative light serves no purpose other than to look good, with its mesmerizing hippy colours and bubbling "lava".

Another trendy "executive toy" that employs light in a purely aesthetic way is the 1960s-style fibre-optic lamp.

▲ There is nothing like candlelight for adding romance to a room. A set of nightlights along the mantlepiece creates instant magic.

▲ The bubbling lava light makes a mesmeric executive toy.

The light shines down hair-thin strands coated with acrylic or fibreglass so that the light is emitted at the end of the strands far from the source. The light is exceptionally cool at the point of emission and can be handled in complete safety. The most common style of fibre-optic lamp features a dome of moving bristles spraying out from a central core that holds the light source. Most have the quirky effect of going through a series of vivid colour changes, producing an almost hypnotic effect.

Neon signs are also making an appearance in contemporary loft-style apartments. Also termed "cold cathode" illumination, neon produces a low level of intensely colourful light that is more commonly used in commercial signs and public displays. It is expensive and needs to be installed by a specialist because it runs on a very high voltage of electricity, but it can be used to highlight architectural features, such as mouldings, to create a strikingly decorative image.

◀ Take a large aluminium bucket full of sand and insert a large number of lit candles for an instant party atmosphere.

hallways

The hallway sets the scene for the rest of your home. It is the first "room" that guests see and should therefore be used to give the right impression. It is vital that the look is stylish and the atmosphere welcoming.

Of course, the hall is not actually a room at all but an entry and exit point where people congregate to say their hellos and goodbyes. It constitutes an area en route from the public world outside to the more intimate rooms within your home. It is therefore important that the light "introduces" guests to your home and welcomes them into the more private areas within.

Most hallways are long and narrow, which sets great limitations on how you can furnish and light them. The floor area, being so limited, reduces the variety of features that can be incorporated. This leaves the emphasis mainly on the walls, the structural details of the space and any architectural features. These should be highlighted wherever possible to emphasize the links with the other rooms, setting the tone, so to speak, of what is to follow.

At the same time, this compact area needs to include practical elements. A mirror is essential for checking your appearance prior to facing the outside world and a cupboard is useful for storing coats before and after venturing out. The hall is also where you will have your entry system if you live in an apartment. For these reasons, the hallway needs, at times, to be clear and bright. Finally, the hall lighting scheme must conform with the style of illumination in the rest of the home, so there are no jarring notes as you move further inside.

As well as hallways, there are often staircases and adjacent landings to be considered. Landings are similar to hallways in that they link various rooms and are seen when people are en route from one place to another. However, they are often more spacious than the hallway and this gives the possibility for more interesting decoration and lighting. You may even be able to isolate an area of the landing for a small desk or window seat. Sometimes a large chest of drawers or a wardrobe can be placed on the landings of larger houses. Increasingly, open-plan living means that these transition areas can be given more emphasis than you might at first think.

▼ For a lighter, airier feel consider replacing a solid front door with a glazed one using toughened security glass.

▼ To maximize on the daylight, hang one wall with a large expanse of mirror to reflect all available light around the room.

Increasing natural daylight

There is nothing as depressing as a dark, gloomy hallway. You will want to ensure that, during the day at least, the hall is naturally well lit to welcome in the outside world. One of the simplest ways to let in more light is to install a glazed front door. The best choice for extra security is heavy-duty glass. Plain or etched glass will allow most light through but, in Victorian and Edwardian houses, stained glass is more common. While coloured glass lets in less light, it can create an attractive effect with dappled jewel tones reflected around the walls. A fan light above the door will also increase the level of natural ambient light. You can adapt the door opening to include this type of window but consult a builder first to check on load-bearing restrictions.

Another way to enhance the effect of daylight is to incorporate glazed doors to the internal rooms. In this way light can be "borrowed" from other rooms that may be better lit than the hallway itself. Neo-Georgian glazed doors can look dated, so for a more stylish look, choose traditional-style French doors – genuine old ones are available at reclamation yards if you are prepared to search for them. Alternatively, look out for reproduction French doors. The best are glazed to just beneath the door handle, with the lower part of the door made from solid wood. If you want an opaque effect, the glass can be painted with a special liquid glass etch, available from hardware stores and artists' supply shops. This will let the light through without allowing callers to see from the hallway into the private rooms beyond.

▲ If you have enough room, and an electrical socket, a hall table with table lamp will create a pleasant, warm welcome.

▲ Glass Turkish lanterns give a gentle, jewel-coloured light for the hall. Consider hanging two or more at different levels as a feature.

Decorate your hallway in bright, airy colours to maximize the effectiveness of the light. Pale cream, white and pastel shades work particularly well. Soft sky blue is a lovely way to enlighten the hallway with the promise of a sunny day outside.

Mirrors undoubtedly have an enormous effect on the feel and look of the light. The larger they are, the better. Sheet mirrors down both sides of the hallway look stunning in a contemporary setting. Large gilded or wooden framed mirrors work on the same principle and will help to reduce a gloomy atmosphere considerably in a period-style hallway. They are also very useful, of course, for checking your appearance before opening the front door to visitors or going outside.

Welcoming lamplight

At its most simple and effective, the hallway can be lit by a single table lamp. For this arrangement you need both a nearby power point and a hallway wide enough to accommodate a slim console table. Bear these requirements in mind if you are rewiring or carrying out any building work. Lamps are an attractive way to light the hall because they give out a warm, glowing light when fitted with a tungsten bulb and create just the right sort of welcoming ambience that a hallway should possess. A table lamp can be used not only after dark but also on dismal winter days. Some designers swear by this device and keep a hall lamp switched on all day, because it is such a warming feature to come home to. Do make sure, however, that the lamp does not protrude into the walkway so that someone could knock it over as they brush past. To avoid this, the best choice of lamp is one with a narrow shade and wide, stable base.

Choosing pendants

Another elementary form of lighting for the hallway is a classic pendant. Traditionally, lantern-style fittings are used, mainly composed of four flat panes of glass held in a gilded frame. These are now available in a variety of updated versions, made from metals such as wrought iron and pewter. If you prefer a more bohemian look, choose a Turkish-style lantern. These generally consist of a glass globe and are available in purple, green, amber, blue and other striking jewel colours. They are particularly impressive at night, when they can help to create a glamorous party atmosphere. However, bear in mind that the coloured glass

▲ If you have pictures on your staircase, light them with the dual purpose of creating both accent and ambient illumination.

will distort the appearance of soft furnishings after dark and may be too overpowering unless fitted with a low-wattage bulb. The best type of bulb to choose is halogen, which gives out a white light with good colour rendering properties; tungsten can look too yellow.

Open, metal-shaded pendants, which are more often associated with kitchen lighting, are also finding their way into modern hallways. Again, these are best fitted with a low-wattage bulb and used as a supplementary rather than main form of lighting. The problem with open pendants is

▼ This long hall has been turned into a gallery by using halogen spots recessed into the ceiling and angled onto a set of canvases.

▲ Create a touch of the theatrical by lighting a simple vase of flowers in an alcove, with a single, narrow-beam downlighter.

that they tend to shine straight down and cast hard shadows over anyone standing beneath them – which is often the only place to stand in a narrow hall. If you have no other form of lighting in your hallway, it is best to opt for an enclosed opaque shade made from glass, paper or plastic, which will produce a softer ambient light. Alternatively, use a silver-crowned reflector bulb that will throw some of the light up towards the ceiling and is therefore less harsh.

On a practical note, remember to place an electrical switch near the front door, so that you can flick the light on easily as soon as you enter the hallway. Similarly, position electrical switches at the top and bottom of the stairs to light the each section of landing.

Lighting pictures

If you would like to hang pictures along the stairway, installing wall lights will serve the dual purpose of creating attractive ambient light while highlighting these decorative details. Wall lights are also a good choice for the stairway because they throw a diffuse light up the walls, which is less likely to dazzle anyone using the stairs. Another way to light paintings or small sculptures is by using low-voltage

halogen downlighters. These can be recessed into the ceiling to reduce glare or can take the form of directable spotlights that can be angled to highlight alcoves, pictures or architectural details.

Lighting can also be used to give a single picture dramatic impact, particularly in a long corridor setting. Place a large, colourful painting at the end of the corridor and highlight it with bright halogen spotlights, leaving the rest of the corridor in semi-darkness. The contrast of bright illumination and semi-darkness will draw attention to the picture and heighten its impact.

The feel-good factor

The hallway is a good place to add a touch of the theatrical to your home, particularly at night. If you have the space, a chandelier – either traditional or more contemporary in design – will create a stunning focus in the hallway and add a sense of drama. Fit the chandelier with multiple low-voltage capsules. These will twinkle in the same way as candlelight and look very effective when shining through the crystal drops of a large chandelier.

An alcove halfway up the staircase provides a wonderful opportunity to create a dramatic lighting display.

▼ Increasingly, modern lights are almost sculptural in their appeal. Designs include paper blocks and curving acrylic towers.

▲ This pair of lights has been simply hung on the wall, just like a painting. They are operated by regular in-line switches.

Anything placed in the alcove can be highlighted with a single spotlight or a recessed downlighter to stunning effect. Even a simple vase of flowers can look almost surreal when backlit, while the textural quality of a small sculpture will be greatly amplified if lit from beneath. The best way to do this is to place a glass shelf in the alcove and conceal a mini-fluorescent tube beneath it. This can be illuminated throughout the day in the same way as a museum display.

If you are holding a party, the hallway is a good place to use candlelight *en masse*. Large, wide candles are a practical choice, since they will burn for a long time and are stable – the result will be even more dramatic if they are scented. As always with lit candles, never leave them unattended and make sure they are well out of the way of people removing their hats and coats.

Decorative lighting

Once you have achieved good-quality ambient lighting in your hallway, you can have some fun with decorative lighting. Some decorative lights are almost works of art in their own right and are now readily available and often reasonably priced. In large, open-spaced halls and

corridors, look for large designs that form, in effect, a sculpture of light. Large, colourless, free-standing columns made of polypropylene, glass or paper are particularly attractive – lit from within by two or more bulbs, they create stunning columns of light.

In a more compact hallway, look for cutting-edge designs that are smaller but still distinctive and stylish. They will add to the level of ambient light and at the same time form highly decorative features in a hallway where there is little room for other adornment. There are many options to choose from – a pair of downlighters mounted on canvas and hung side-by-side, beaded ceramic uplighters, glass and pearl wall lights or a rusted floral chandelier are just a few examples of the multitude available.

Lighting the stairs

For practical reasons the staircase needs to be well lit at all times, to illuminate the tread and reduce the risk of tripping or falling. Choose a similar style of lighting to that used in the entrance hall, to create a sense of continuity.

You can integrate lighting into the staircase itself to create a strikingly modern effect. Low-voltage halogen reflectors set into the sides of the staircase are particularly

◄ Tiny halogen spotlights set into the side of these steps are used to light the way and also enhance the texture of the rough stone.

▲ This passageway of reinforced glass is lit from beneath with fluorescent tubes so that the effect is like walking on water.

▲ Square holes cut into the risers of these steps and lit by fluorescent tubes create a smart design feature.

opaque acrylic covers. Fluorescent tubes are highly economical and energy efficient, so they are particularly suitable for dark staircases where they can be switched on all the time. They have a life of around 8,000 hours, which reduces the effort of having to replace the bulbs, and give out a cool, white light that is perfect for lighting most types of wooden staircases.

Into the future

At its most contemporary, lighting can be combined with a glass staircase to stunning effect. Glass floors and staircases are constructed from sections of glass, which can be lit from beneath with a series of fluorescent tubes. The result is an amazing, futuristic staircase of light – mounting such a staircase feels rather like walking on water. Marble or glass-clad walls further accentuate this sensation, especially when combined with concealed uplighters washing the top half of the wall with light.

To illuminate a dark upstairs landing, look out for so-called "sun pipe" fittings, which can be fitted into the roof and reflect daylight into the landing using a ceiling diffuser and internal mirrors. They are a great way to introduce light into a windowless or gloomy area.

effective on stone or wooden stairs – the lights pick out the textures of the materials and reflect off the surfaces to produce a warm-coloured glow.

You can also set lights into the risers of a wooden staircase. Set mini-fluorescent strips into square or round holes on the vertical of the tread and conceal them behind

living rooms

The living room is the heart of the home – we spend more waking hours here than in any other room. It is a multi-purpose space in which we congregate with members of the household as well as entertain guests, so it has to look good enough to impress visitors and neighbours.

Most of us spend a lot of money and effort furnishing our living rooms, and lighting is an important part of that investment. Yet with so much choice in the shops, and so little guidance, it can be difficult to know where to start.

The living room lighting design should be versatile. It must provide the right lighting environment for a number of activities which, particularly in the contemporary home, may be quite diverse. This room is where you will settle down to read in peace, perhaps play chess or spend time with your children. You will certainly want to relax and unwind, put your feet up, entertain and watch television in your living room. Each of these activities requires a different atmosphere and mood, and lighting will be an invaluable tool in achieving this.

A good starting point is to list the different needs that your living room must fulfil and then consider what sort of lighting plan would best suit each activity. As well as practical considerations, you should think about style and aesthetics. Ambient lighting, particularly, will have a strong influence on the character of the room. If used well, you can exploit the ambient light to transform an unsympathetic area into a sensuous and uplifting one, by virtue of contrasting and complimentary light sources. If the room has attractive architectural features, you can highlight them with specific illumination, as well as any interesting alcoves and recesses.

Remember that the living room is also the room in which you are likely to display your favourite books, paintings and other treasured objects. These will take pride of place and require the appropriate type of lighting if they are to retain their impact, particularly in the evening after dark. You will also need to plan some directional task lighting near chairs and sofas to provide focused lighting for reading.

▼ Make the most of large floor-to-ceiling windows by using an airy expanse of pure white cotton voile.

▲ If you do go for traditional drapes, choose plain, light colours to maintain a cool contemporary feeling.

Making the most of natural light

Assessing the level of ambient, or background, lighting is the first consideration in planning for your living room. It is vital to create a relaxing backdrop onto which you can overlay other types of lighting. Most fundamental of all is natural light and how to enhance it. A living room that faces north or north-east will have a cool, bluish light, very different from a south-facing room, which will benefit from richer, golden tones. Of course, you cannot alter the orientation of your home, but you *can* change the way in which you use the space.

Relocate the living room to the first floor, where it will be less in shadow from surrounding trees and buildings, and it will immediately profit from a lighter, sunnier feel. The bedrooms, which will be used mostly after dark, can be relegated to the ground floor, where the natural light is more restricted. It is this kind of lateral thinking that sets lighting designers and architects apart and can dramatically shape the environment in which you live.

Working with windows

The more windows, or light sources, you have, the better the quality of the ambient light in the room. Lit by just a single window, the room will suffer from extremes of light and shade. You may find that the room is very bright near the window and heavily in shadow or even gloomy at the far end. If possible, install extra windows, taking care to position them to allow maximum light into the room.

Windows set into the ceiling have a marvellous effect on the levels of light in a room, producing constant illumination throughout the day and a clear, airy mood that even the most expensive lighting scheme cannot replicate. Similarly, replacing a casement with French windows will achieve greater floor-to-ceiling illumination and improve the penetration of light into the room.

If your living room is naturally dark, you may have no choice but to switch the lights on during the daytime. Alternatively, consider replacing a solid partition with glass bricks, to borrow light from an adjacent area.

Window treatments

Your choice of window treatment can dramatically alter the quality and quantity of light that enters the living room. In a large, naturally well-lit room, decorated all in white, a single plain navy curtain draped across one window can look dramatic and stylish, without plunging

▼ A plain casement window makes the most of the natural light. Fit an acrylic panel over it to maintain privacy.

▲ These bright orange and pink window panels tint the cool city light as it filters through the windows of this modern loft.

▼ This retro-style voile with its 1960s cube design offers exactly the right combination of colour and transparency.

the room into shadow. However, avoid hanging drapes that obscure the window frame if the living room is dark or north-facing – unless you are prepared to light the room artificially at all times.

If your living room is not overlooked by neighbours, leaving a large window completely unadorned and letting the daylight flood in is an attractive prospect. This minimalist style is increasingly finding favour with modern designers, who have had their fill of fussy swags and drapes. Another modern alternative is to use etched or translucent glass, which gently diffuses and filters bright sunlight without reducing its intensity. A more contemporary look, but similar in effect, is the use of semi-opaque plastic laminates to cover whole window casements. Semi-transparent voile panels are easier to fit in place and even more versatile – an excellent way to maintain privacy without blocking out sunlight.

For a different effect altogether, try hanging coloured muslins, a ploy frequently used by designers to change the quality of the natural light. Depending on the shade you choose, they can transform daylight into a subtle, honey glow or produce an intense concentration of colour that will envelop your whole living room.

Multiple light sources

Another clever way to create flattering ambient light is to use indirect illumination, created by multiple light sources and reflected around the room. This will suit the needs of anyone using the room for various activities, but can also create a relaxing setting for those who want to sit back and relax or listen to soft music.

Concealed lighting is particularly effective in the living room. The light sources, such as the new generation of mini-fluorescent strips, can be positioned neatly behind cornicing or high cabinets. With this type of installation, the light is directed up towards the ceiling and then reflected back into the room, creating an even level of ambient light, devoid of harsh shadows.

You can produce the same effect in alcoves using unobtrusive wall washers, which utilize the wall itself as a reflector. These fittings can be attached to the wall, mounted on tracks or recessed into the surface for a more permanent fixing. The effect is one of loftiness and space and is well suited to slick, contemporary living rooms. Make sure your walls are smooth and immaculate enough to bear up to the scrutiny of this type of lighting though, and take care not to position the washers too near a table or chairs where they could dazzle. Multiple eyeball spots that can swivel in their sockets, and therefore be tilted and moved as required, are an effective type of wall washer. They are often employed to light a wall of pictures while subtly contributing to the level of background light.

Positioning furniture

The way you position furniture in the living room is also critical. It can alter the way that light enters through windows and also change how it is reflected and bounced around the room. You may want to place a large sofa in front of the window – to allow more floor space elsewhere in the room – but in a dark room this may block out so much natural light as to be totally impractical. Light and interior decor should never be considered in isolation. Try to leave as much space as possible around chairs, and light the room with floor-to-ceiling illumination to engender a feeling of spaciousness.

Choosing soft furnishings

The quality of the light will alter the appearance of the soft furnishings that you choose for your living room. Cool tones of blue, grey and green that are refreshing in a well-lit room can become downright dull in a poorly lit, north-facing one. To enhance the appearance of natural light in a dimly lit room, consider using sunny tones from the yellow palette to "warm" the light.

Your choice of wall and ceiling colours will also have a direct effect on the amount of artificial lighting the room

will need. Rich, dark shades, such as terracotta, absorb light and require a high-intensity lighting plan, with plenty of tungsten lamps to produce a warm ambience after dark. By contrast, a contemporary-style room, decorated in soft pastels or white, is better lit with low-voltage halogen lights, as such pale colours can take on an unattractive, even "dirty" tinge under tungsten bulbs.

Consider using colours that change in different lights – parchment, for example, is pale cream in daylight yet turns golden in the yellowy radiance of tungsten light at night. It is nearly always the case that designers and lighting experts choose pure white for the ceiling. This is in order to make the most of natural light in the daytime and to act as an antidote to the yellow cast of tungsten lighting.

Choosing light fittings

When planning the lighting for your living room, making sure that the fittings are sympathetic to the design of the room is as important as the positioning of them. But things are not always what they seem. In a contemporary living room, a period-style wall sconce can be successfully combined with modern wall patterns. Conversely, a traditional room with ornate architectural features can benefit from low-voltage spotlights, floor-standing uplighters and perhaps a striking architectural pendant as a main focus.

Low-voltage lighting supported on tracks or on unsheathed wire (so-called "bare wire" installations) looks dramatic, especially if suspended at different heights. Such sculptural effects look good in all types of settings.

Central pendants

Traditionally, living rooms were lit by a single pendant light hanging in the centre of the room and this is still often the case. These are the bane of most lighting designers' lives, as they create a wide pool of glaring light immediately beneath the bulb and leave the recesses and corners of the room in gloom. The quality of the light is poor – ineffectual at best and depressing at worst. At the flick of a switch the mood of the room is shattered, all atmopshere is lost. Instead of intimate contrasts of light and shade in different quarters of the room, there is one bland, lifeless flood.

In older houses, the pendant light has nevertheless remained a fixture, if only due to the ornate plaster roses that adorn the centre of the ceiling and would look oddly

▶ The latest low voltage halogen lights can be suspended on bare wires and even strung vertically for a sculptural effect.

▶▶ Traditional and modern style blend perfectly in this living room with its chic block walls and chandelier-style wall lights.

▼ Invest in multiple light sources and you will be rewarded by an engaging quality of light throughout the day and night.

▼ This standard lamp takes up minimal floor space, yet incorporates a small round sofa table for books and flowers.

▼ Multiple light sources can include a collection of lamps. Vary the wattage of each bulb to create a different emphasis.

▼ Modern interpretations of chandeliers feature mini halogen capsules that throw out tiny sparkles of starlight.

▼ This Turkish-style lantern will glow a delicate shade of blue when lit with a mains voltage halogen bulb.

redundant without the standard central light suspended from them. There are, however, some very attractive central fittings – chandeliers, for instance – that have never lost their appeal. Indeed, chandeliers have recently enjoyed a resurgence of popularity with modern lighting designers, who have adapted them to suit late-20th-century tastes. Contemporary chandelier designs feature ornate, twisted metal arms bearing jewel-coloured glass drops that sprinkle gemstone shades about the room. Some chandelier designs have been adapted to take low-voltage halogen capsules, whose tiny, bright white light enhances the sparkling effect of the glass.

If you want to keep your pendant fitting, the solution is to incorporate it into a more sophisticated lighting scheme, rather than leave it as the only source of illumination in your living room. Another important point is to reduce the power of the pendant light so that it blends into the overall lighting plan rather than allowing it to dominate the room. The use of low-wattage bulbs and enclosed shades will also help to soften the light from a pendant fitting. The result will be gentle enough not to overwhelm the subtler, more attractive output of table lamps and uplighters.

▼ So much more sophisticated than a single pendant, here halogen spot lights and lamps create a combined ambient light.

▲ Intimate lamp light and illumination at floor level prevents this modern, white interior from appearing too clinical.

▲ Less is more when it comes to good display. Here, small halogen downlights illuminate a discreet collection of glass.

Lighting displays

You can witness the effectiveness of good display lighting by walking into any modern department store or boutique where the items are carefully lit to best effect. We can all learn from such displays when lighting sculpture, books or other favourite objects in our own living rooms. Low-voltage halogen lights are the best method of accenting small items with precise, narrow beams of twinkling light. They are compact and unobtrusive, yet deliver a crisp white light with excellent colour fidelity. However, bear in mind that the angle and direction of accent lighting is crucial to success and that obtrusive lighting can actually draw attention away from the item you are trying to highlight.

Illuminated glass shelving is frequently seen in contemporary settings for displaying objects. The shelves can be lit from above or below, with spots concealed within the base or ceiling of the unit, to make a striking impact. The treasures on display seem almost to float in the illuminated space. Lit from the sides, the light creates interesting lateral shadows and is particularly effective for objects with pleasing texture and form. Meanwhile, at a simpler level, clip-on spotlights can make easy work of selecting CDs, books and magazines from shelves.

▼ Lighting can go beyond mere illumination and become visual art in its own right – as shown with this paper light scultpture.

▲ Often the last consideration, candles can add a sense of well-being and occasssion to a living room.

Creating space with light

With careful planning, lighting can be used to conjure all sorts of clever tricks that can make a small living room seem much larger than it really is. Uplighters are an excellent way to achieve this – the light bounces off the ceiling and walls and so creates a greater sense of space. This feeling of space can be further enhanced by moving the sofas and chairs a little way from the walls and placing light sources behind them. Painting the ceiling white or a light pastel shade will create an illusion of greater height that will make the room feel less confining. Use uplighters to highlight architectural ceiling features such as mouldings and cornicing to emphasize the illusion.

By contrast, in the wrong setting, uplighters can produce an empty, cavernous feeling, almost clinical in effect, particularly in modern, high-ceilinged living spaces. To prevent a spacious room from resembling an airport waiting lounge, carefully position lower level lighting. This can be at floor level, recessed into the walls or, in its simplest form, in the shape of floor or table lamps placed near armchairs and sofas. Such discreet use of lamps is an effective device for dividing a large living room into several smaller areas.

Lighting as decoration

In a contemporary living room, where the illumination has been reduced to hi-tech minimal spots and low-voltage reflectors, lighting comes into its own as a form of decoration. Some modern lights use such low-power bulbs that they do not function as practical light sources – the tiny sparkles they emit transform the light itself into an illuminated sculpture and therein lies their appeal. Many modern light designs have achieved a status over and above that of mere "lights".

The flickering candle

At its most basic level, decorative lighting can simply be the flicker of a live flame. Even the most mundane lighting schemes can be enhanced by the warmth of burning candles or a blazing log fire. To appreciate the real flames, dim the electric lights down low and bask in the sparkling sensuality of the dancing reflections. Amassing candles of different sizes around the room, in nooks and crannies, will create a spiritual sense of well-being and act as an intense feel-good factor. Above all else, candlelight or firelight is immensely flattering and the perfect accompaniment to celebrations, parties and intimate occasions.

▲ The latest high-tech track lighting is highly flexible, Each lamp can be moved up and down the track and angled at will.

▲ In a modern apartment with cavernous, high ceilings, these low-level, Japanese-style paper lamps add a welcome intimacy.

Keep it flexible

In some penthouse apartments, freeform tracks snake across the ceiling, punctuated by transformers and dotted with a large number of lights. This creates an infinitely flexible scheme that is nothing if not glamorous. In fact, as an area that has to accommodate so many different activities, *all* living rooms should feature flexible lighting – and this does not have to mean loft-style tracking. There will probably be times when you need to move your furniture around – you may want to reposition chairs and small tables when visitors arrive, or alter the way in which you use your living space if your lifestyle changes. For all these reasons, portable fittings such as table lamps, standard lamps and free-standing uplighters are extremely useful in the living area. They can be unplugged easily and moved around to create intimate rings of light in the desired places, and can help to define different areas of the room in an instant.

Lamplight

Lamps are the key ingredient in a flexible living room lighting scheme. Easy to incorporate, they add to the background light while also highlighting focal areas of the room – a coffee table, a comfortable chair for reading or an elegant sofa, for example. Above all, lamps create a sense of warm intimacy and have a sympathetic allure; they really are indispensable, whatever the style of the room. A clinically white living room will benefit immensely from a collection of stylish lamps, switched on even in daylight. These add a permanent glow of tungsten to the room, which is actually just a shade paler than candlelight. With this in mind, it is always sensible to have a number of electrical sockets installed if you have the chance, so that flexes can be neatly hidden should you decide to change the position of the furniture.

The height of the lamp and the colour of the shade play a crucial role in the effect produced. The lower the lamp, the more intimate the atmosphere; the darker the shade, the deeper the mood. Some shades are black on the outside with a gold lining on the inside, so that the light cannot penetrate sideways but only fall in a golden pool beneath the shade. These, in particular, create an intensely private setting.

Simply changing the shade on a lamp can create dramatically different looks, both in terms of the light that is thrown out and the style of the fitting. High-fashion

▼ The current trend for beading has even left it's mark on lighting styles. Here 1920s-style lamps create a delicate, feminine effect.

▼ Task lights are becoming more and more common in living rooms – as the contemporary alternative to traditional lamps.

treatments include fake fur, velvet and even leather shades. Beaded fringing around the base of shades, which originally became popular in the 1920s, has also found favour with modern designers, who revel in the way the light trickles through the beads and kaleidoscopes around the room. In a traditional living room, pairs of lamps are usually employed, flanking a sofa or fireplace.

Floor lamp solutions

If you are short of space, floor lamps are a practical alternative to table lamps, since they require no surface on which to be placed. Situated immediately beside or behind an armchair, they are the perfect way to deliver localized light for reading. Like table lamps, they are flexible, portable and increasingly available in modern materials such as frosted glass and acrylics to give out a clean, pure illumination. Most of all, floor lamps have a majestic appeal and create an engaging focus of interest in the living room, where everything tends to be on the same horizontal plane. Look out for simple, modern designs, which often have fine metal stems and adjustable Anglepoise-style shades. They fit in perfectly with the twin contemporary themes of minimalism and practicality.

Reading lights

Not just the preserve of the study or workroom, task lights are creeping more and more into the modern living room, often in the form of practical, no-nonsense designs. The criteria is that they should be fully directional, flexible and versatile. The latest hi-tech designs are all of these things and they also blend surprisingly well with both period and modern interiors. Some are designed to take low-voltage halogen bulbs and have chic blue or green glass shades, while at the cheapest end of the spectrum are simple tungsten lamps with flexible stems. Fashionable, business-like designs are more expensive but their height and angle can be adjusted with cantilevered or tensioned arms.

If you choose spotlights to read by, these will take the form of a permanent fixture and cannot be moved easily should you decide to rearrange the furniture. However, they are a neat solution for a more compact living space, though you must make sure that they are not too bright. When choosing the type of lighting you want to read by, remember that excessively bright illumination will create a huge contrast between the ambient light and that reflected from the page of your book. This is likely to cause eyestrain and even headaches.

Watching television

The same rules apply when you are watching television. You should not view the screen in the dark; the bright and flickering light source of the television requires intense concentration and repetitive eye adjustment. If the contrast between the bright screen and the darkened room is too great, your eyes will become tired and you risk developing headaches. Conversely, if the ambient light is too bright, or if there is a shaft of daylight directed at the screen, it will be almost impossible to see the television picture properly. The ideal environment for watching television is diffuse ambient light, at about the same brightness level as that of the screen itself, because it reduces the contrast in lighting levels to a minimum.

Lighting pictures

Pictures and paintings need careful consideration when designing your living room lighting scheme. After dark, without the right sort of illumination, pictures can become almost indiscernible and lose all their impact, colour and visual appeal. Go to any gallery and you will see state-of-the-art ideas for how to light pictures. Restaurants, museums and chic retail outlets are also good sources of inspiration. One of the best solutions for lighting pictures and paintings in a contemporary living room is low-voltage halogen lighting, with a clean, direct point of light emanating from a discrete fitting; the best choices are spotlights that deliver a precise, narrow beam. Some have an integral tilting mechanism for easy positioning and accuracy. Eyeball spotlights create a broader beam of light and are useful for collections of several small pictures rather than one focal canvas.

For classic interiors, a contemporary wrought-iron uplighter together with a floor light set beneath the pictures can flood them with an even, warm tungsten illumination and minimize glare. During the day, the uplighter alone can be switched on. Choose a fitting that can be dimmed.

The traditional arrangement in which a light is extended on arms in front of or above the picture is now available in a range of modern chrome and glass fittings. The light should be almost as wide as the picture and extend far enough out to flood the whole frame with light.

◄ Pictures can be amassed on a wall and then lit with a floor lamp placed nearby and wall lights for a cosy, relaxed effect.

◄◄ Never watch television in the dark. Instead you should aim to create a diffuse ambient light of the same intensity as the screen.

kitchens

The kitchen performs two functions. Primarily, it is a place for storing, preparing and cooking food and requires a bright, clean light with emphasis on work surfaces, hob, sink and oven. Secondly, it is a place where guests and family come together, which requires relaxed, warm lighting. Reconciling these two requirements is vital for successful kitchen lighting. The contemporary kitchen has become the new centre for entertaining, a room in which people gather to eat and enjoy each other's company in an informal setting. However, it is important not to place aesthetics over practical considerations.

With the trend for open-plan living spaces, kitchen lighting should be every bit as good as the lighting in the rest of the home – if not better. The intensity and colour of the lighting should match, or at least be similar to, that in other areas of the home. This will avoid an unpleasant jarring effect when you enter the room; above all, you should not be dazzled by a harsh, utilitarian glare.

The lighting must also be easily controllable, so that you can adapt it in accordance with the natural light levels at various times of the day as well as create the required atmosphere at the flick of a switch.

We have come a long way from the single pendant light or fluorescent strip that was once the main form of kitchen illumination. Nowadays, the same rule applies to lighting kitchens as to other rooms in the home: it is vital to layer different light sources so that you can achieve the subtle changes required for different activities.

Surface-mounted lights, track lighting down the centre of the ceiling or a grid format of low-voltage halogen lights all present the same problems – they cast harsh, unflattering shadows over the kitchen and the people in it. Avoid these problems by starting with good, bright ambient light and combining it with effective illumination of the work surfaces, hob and sink. This should be overlaid with warm, atmospheric tones of tungsten, particularly in the eating area. And just because this is the kitchen, it does not mean you cannot install some decorative architectural uplighters with warm tungsten bulbs to finish the scheme. These are important finishing touches to be added once you have taken care of all the practical lighting requirements.

▲ The layout of your kitchen should dictate your lighting scheme.
Here two pendant lights compliment good natural illumination.

Where to start

The best ploy when designing a kitchen lighting scheme
is to begin with your functional requirements – get your
ambient and task lighting right and you can then go on to
choose the details, such as accent and decorative lighting.
Unless you are lucky enough to be starting from scratch,
you will have to work around existing kitchen units and
fixtures. Even in a free-form kitchen, where there are no
fitted units, you will be hampered by considerations such
plumbing and the position of electrical points. It is around
the main working elements of the kitchen that you will be
basing your lighting scheme, namely the hob, oven and
sink. In contrast to living rooms, where the name of the
game is flexibility, most lighting in the kitchen will be fixed,
so positioning your lights in the right places is crucial.

Your kitchen layout

If you are starting from scratch and have the opportunity
to design your kitchen layout, it is vital to orientate the
room correctly, in relation to the lighting. In a dark room,
consider how to enhance the natural light as much as
possible; you can add good-quality artificial daylight in the
form of multiple low-voltage halogen lights to produce a

clear, bright white light – when it is sunny and bright
outside, there is nothing more depressing than working in
a gloomy kitchen.

These days, two rooms are often joined together to
create a large kitchen that includes a dining area or
breakfast bar. Again, it is preferable if this area is naturally
lit, ideally by large French windows with access to a garden
or roof terrace. Before you choose the units, decide how
you might increase the amount of daylight, perhaps by
enlarging a window, removing a dividing wall, installing a
skylight or choosing an all-white scheme.

How it was

Back in the 1950s, when the fitted kitchen was first
introduced, housewives were most likely to be cooking
under the glare of a fluorescent tube (devised in the
1930s). Although this type of lighting was economical and
hailed at the time as "the latest thing", it emitted a harsh
light that gave everything in its wake an unhealthy pallor.
This was true for the food as well as the families who
unhappily had to eat under such conditions.

Fluorescent light has dramatic peaks in the greenish-
yellow and orange part of the colour spectrum that distort

▼ Clean white walls and pale wood make the most of the natural light here. A Shaker-style candelabra lights the table at night.

▼ This lofty kitchen is flooded with natural daylight, while a pair uplighters on the wall highlight the old wooden ceiling beams.

▼ This new kitchen extension benefits from a generous strip of skylights over the worksurface to make the most of the daylight.

the colour of food in an unacceptable way. This makes it difficult to assess the condition of fresh food and gives prepared meals an unappetizing appearance. Add to that the delay in the light coming on and the flickery quality and hum of the tubes, and the fluorescent light finally became unacceptable in most household kitchens.

Making the most of daylight

During the daytime the ideal ambient light is, of course, daylight – and lots of it. There is nothing more enjoyable than preparing food in a kitchen where natural light is flooding through a large picture window or, better still, through French doors, with a fresh herb garden beyond. Back in the real world, even if you live in a built-up city, try to get as much natural light into your kitchen as possible. Dispense with window treatments, unless you are overlooked by neighbours and need your privacy. A good solution is to install etched glass, which will allow as much light into the room as possible while blocking the view into the room. If you have a flat roof, incorporate a large skylight in your plans. This will be a useful addition to the level of ambient light and, coming from above, will illuminate a far greater area than a vertical window.

▼ Keep the colour scheme monochrome and add clean, white low voltage halogen spots for a contemporary look.

Artificial ambient light

Kitchens need a fairly high level of good ambient lighting, supplemented by specific task lighting over the work surfaces, sink, hob and other key food preparation areas. In perfect conditions the quality of the light should be even and devoid of shadows. It is important that when arranging food at the work surface the cook is not standing in his or her own light, and there should be no gloomy nooks and crannies where visibility is a problem. Safety is paramount, given that the average kitchen contains naked flames, heat, boiling water, steam and sharp knives, so a high level of bright, clear light is essential to minimize the risk of accidents.

Low-voltage halogen lighting, with its bright white quality, is the best choice for simulating natural daylight. Even now, with modern developments in fluorescent lighting where the quality of the illumination is warmer and more hospitable, fluorescent tubes should not be the main light source in the kitchen. The colour rendering is still poor, particularly compared with low-voltage halogen

▼ Downlighters fixed beneath kitchen wall units will flood the worksurface with light – perfect for food preparation.

▼ These so-called "chopstick-style" low voltage halogen downlighters are stylishly suspended between a pair of bare wires.

lighting. However, fluorescents are useful as part of a larger lighting scheme, where they can be used to create a cool, bright, diffuse background light. A good place to install fluorescents is above wall units, where their light can be reflected back off the ceiling.

Fixed lighting

Unlike in the living room, where the key is versatility, in the kitchen the most appropriate types of light fittings are fixed, since much of the furniture in the kitchen is permanently fitted in place. You will want to keep the maximum amount of floor and work surface space free in order to move around easily and prepare food, so there simply is not room to add free-standing table lamps or floor lamps. Also, of course, someone could trip over electrical flexes or cables lying on the floor. In any case, even in the best-kept household, the kitchen is likely to become cluttered and steamy and attract dust and grease, which would making cleaning decorative lamps practically impossible. This leaves you with a choice of downlighters, uplighters, hidden fluorescent mini-tubes and perhaps the odd decorative pendant.

Choosing downlighters

Downlighters come in a huge range of fittings designed to direct light down into the room from a high position – perfect for lighting a kitchen work surface. Small and neat

in design, downlighters have long been used in commercial and retail situations to light displays efficiently. In recent years, they have become the first choice for bathrooms and kitchens where neat, unobtrusive fittings are required, along with excellent light quality. However, being very bright and fairly static, you should position downlighters with care, to avoid glare. Dimming is a possibility, but this can reduce the level of lighting to such a point that it is not practical.

Kitchen downlighters may be partially or wholly recessed, surface-mounted or even set on wires or high-tech tracks. They can also be fixed or directional, which is useful for illuminating specific work areas or subtly changing the emphasis of a mainly static lighting scheme. You can also choose from wide or narrow beams, and traditional tungsten or low-voltage halogen – the choice is virtually endless.

Fully recessed downlighters require a space cavity in the ceiling of at least 12.5cm (5in) to accommodate the fitting and to ensure adequate ventilation. If there is not enough space, the alternative is to have the lights ceiling-mounted. In any case, all downlighters should have heatproof covers fitted over the terminals to avoid the risk of fire; low-voltage halogen lights, in particular, get extremely hot. It is advisable to have them fitted by a fully qualified electrician, who will ensure correct installation and adequate ventilation.

▼ The working area in this small kitchen benefits from natural light together with downlighters above the sink.

▼ Today's stainless steel kitchens give multiple reflections from a series of downlighters. Choose flexible fittings for extra versatility.

The joy of downlighters is that they are so discrete, particularly the tiny low-voltage halogen fittings. Another advantage is that they are "timeless", so they suit both traditional and modern kitchen designs. Remember that downlighters tend to throw most of their light onto the horizontal surfaces beneath them, leaving vertical surfaces such as walls and unit fronts less well lit. This means you will need further light sources to "fill in" and warm the sometimes stark light quality. Also note that rows and rows of ceiling fittings can give the modern kitchen a rather utilitarian feel, so opt for directional lights that can shine onto walls and units, producing a less regimented lighting arrangement. If the kitchen has a warm colour scheme, such as pale wood units or coloured walls, the light reflected off these surfaces and around the room will have a softer quality than it would have in a white scheme.

Do not ignore the versatility of directional downlighters. You can use them as accent lights to highlight a row of spice jars or rack of utensils, or to throw reflections and refractions off coloured glass bottles. Remember that low-voltage halogen downlighters do not have to be limited to lighting work surfaces in the kitchen; they can also be used to light more decorative areas.

▲ Use a directional spotlight to highlight a collection of coloured glass; group of stainless utensils, or series of storage jars.

▲ A good effect can be assured by combining a set of tungsten pendants with low voltage task lights mounted on the walls.

Tungsten or low-voltage halogen?

The choice between traditional tungsten and low-voltage halogen is not simply a matter of style. In almost all kitchens, the clean, cool, bright light of halogen makes it the perfect choice for ambient lighting because it is as near to natural daylight as it is possible to achieve artificially. Low-voltage halogen light can also be used to highlight areas that other types of lighting are unable to reach. Another advantage is the good colour fidelity, which is so important when examining and assessing fresh produce in preparation for cooking,and when checking if food is fully cooked. The bulb wattages of low-halogen lights are also

generally lower than those of tungsten lights, and they have an extended life of around 3,000 hours, so they can be cheaper to operate. However, bear in mind that low-voltage halogen fittings are more expensive than their tungsten equivalents and require transformers, some of which may be bulky.

The crisp white quality of halogen light is also a perfect foil for the materials used in the modern kitchen – white walls, pale wood and stainless steel. If you find that glare is a problem, you can install dimmer switches, although these are best used in rooms where decorative lighting is the focus rather than in the functional lighting of the kitchen.

▼ The sophisticated quality of light in this kitchen is due to the trio of low voltage downlighters flooding onto the wooden blind.

▼ For a modern twist on the traditional pendant light suspended over the kitchen table – this modern halogen version is perfect.

Instead it is easier to replace the existing halogen capsules with slightly lower wattage ones. Always check, when replacing a capsule, that the new one is not too high a wattage for the ceiling fittings and transformers or it could constitute a fire risk.

A common temptation when installing low-voltage halogen downlighters is to put in too many fittings to compensate for the fact that they are so small. This is a mistake, both from the visual and practical point of view. Visually, the resulting light may be dazzlingly bright;

practically, many fittings will create an enormous amount of heat and could even be a fire risk. Always consult a lighting expert when installing low-voltage halogen lighting. He or she will work out how many fittings you need to light the volume of space in your kitchen.

For more traditional-style kitchens, with wooden floors and coloured walls, a combination of different types of light can be used. A stylish choice is to light the kitchen table with one or more low-level pendants, suspended from the ceiling. This will create a warm ambient light,

▲ Here, four tungsten pendants throw a warm light over the sociable area of the kitchen, while halogen lights the work area.

▶ Even the most functional storage jars look decorative when lit well and displayed on smart, glass shelving.

while static, low-voltage downlighters can be used to illuminate units, dressers or even the work surfaces with the pure white halogen light that is ideal for food preparation and cooking.

Lighting work surfaces

Kitchens lack practical, horizontal surfaces on which to position light sources, even though you will need those surfaces to be well lit. To get around this problem, designers often set lights underneath the kitchen wall units. At its most basic, this can simply mean installing small fluorescent tubes at intervals around the kitchen. However, even the new-generation fluorescent lights, while providing bright illumination, have poor colour rendering, which means they are not the best choice for food preparation.

Instead, you could opt for mains-voltage tungsten tubes, which have a warmer tone. However, they are not really bright enough to light a work surface, even if you choose multiple, clear glass bulbs of high wattage. In any case, most fittings specify a maximum of 60 watts.

The best option, therefore, is to fit low-voltage halogen spots. Although this is the most expensive form of kitchen

lighting, its qualities make it much the best source of light, being white, bright and easily directable. The fittings are also extremely small. A typical halogen spot is held in a frame that is set just 5cm (2in) into the cupboard surface with an access hole 7.5cm (3in) wide.

Ceiling downlighters, if directable, can also be shone onto work surfaces, but take care that you are not standing in your own light.

Lighting eating areas

If you plan to eat in your kitchen, lighting can be a good way to separate the eating area from the area devoted to cooking. Just by turning off, or dimming, the bright overhead halogen lights, you can alter the mood of the room. Go on to highlight the dining table with candles or pendant lighting and you can almost make the working part of the kitchen disappear.

Pendant lights take many forms and, depending on the material from which they are made, they create a variety of different effects. Large opaque shades, made from pressed steel, for example, will direct all the light downwards onto the surface below. If they are positioned low over the table or breakfast bar, they create an intimate atmosphere that

► This work surface is lit both by halogen lights recessed under the shelf and by an elegant series of halogen ceiling pendants.

encourages people to lean in towards each other and become enveloped in the warm tungsten glow. Choose open, wide-dished pendants fitted with crown-silvered bulbs. This type of bulb throws the light up into the shade, which then reflects the light down onto the table, thus helping to prevent glare.

In contrast, clear, ribbed, cast-glass shades act rather like a lens, allowing the light to shine both through and below the shade. Some of the light will also be bounced up towards the ceiling to create a good level of ambient light. A row of small pendants with white opaque or coloured shades can look very modern, while shades in glass or metal where the bulb is fully recessed give an attractively soft light. Many pendants come with rise and fall attachments that enable you to adjust their height. Pulling them down to lower the light source immediately creates a more focused and intimate atmosphere.

Lighting cupboards

A practical option is to install light fittings within your kitchen cupboards. When you open them the light will come on, just as it does in the refrigerator. This is extremely useful, especially if you have deep recessed cupboards and are trying to locate something hidden at the back.

If you like the idea of creating a kitchen with atmosphere, choose units that have glass doors so that the light inside can be switched on at any time to shine through and illuminate the room. Modern units often take the form of an almost unadorned run of opaque glass with hidden handles. When these are lit from within, they resemble a giant sheet of light that creates a wonderful gleaming ambience. A simpler method is to install mini-fluorescent or tungsten strips in the "ceiling" of the cupboards. Alternatively, when planning your kitchen, look out for units that are fitted with internal low-voltage halogen lamps that throw light onto the stored contents from either above or behind. These have the dual function of being both practical storage areas and artistic showcases. They look particularly effective if filled with a collection of gleaming modern glass.

On a more modest scale, wooden units with plain glazed doors can contribute extensively to the ambient lighting of the room. The light reflected off the doors produces a welcome warmth that offsets the clear, bright light of massed halogen downlighters.

► Etched glass unit doors let through a subtle ambient light when lit by small halogen bulbs from within.

▲ Without the sparkling quality of halogen lighting, this bank of dark charcoal grey units could look rather gloomy.

Bad lighting can make us ill at ease, but clever, sympathetic lighting can bring a room to life with colour, texture and definition. Even though the kitchen is primarily a working room, try to incorporate as much feel-good factor as you would in the living room – perhaps even more, as the modern family often converges on the kitchen as the main focus of home life and entertaining.

Lighting the hob and cooker

It is vital that the hob and cooker are properly illuminated. Many modern hobs now have a matching hood above, fitted with an integral strip light, adjacent to the extractor fan. This light tends to be operated automatically on pulling out the extractor. In most cases the strip is very small and contains a low-wattage tungsten source that bathes the hob area in a warm glow. However, this is not the ideal light source for checking whether food that is being cooked on the hob is ready. An alternative is to

◄ Lighting of the hob area is particularly important. Here low voltage halogen bulbs form an integral part of the unit.

▼ Look out for the new generation of smart chrome spot light fittings that will supplement your general lighting scheme.

▲ This neat uplighter was simply inserted into the soil of a potted herb which was growing in a metal paint kettle.

install a stainless steel extractor hood over the hob and to fit it with a pair of low-voltage halogen downlighters that will flood the cooking area with clean, bright light.

If you have no hood, install a low-voltage halogen spot in the ceiling immediately above the hob. The best fitting is a directable spot, so that you can illuminate the required area precisely and not just the floor area immediately in front of the hob. It is important to ensure that in this situation you are not standing in your own light.

Other light sources

Many kitchen manufacturers supply their own light fittings, either integral to the units or separately to be used in various places where additional light may be of benefit – both practically and decoratively. These may take the form of elegant downlighter units that are decorative features in their own right and can be mounted on various surfaces around the kitchen. There is also a trend for lights set into canopies that extend from the top of the units over the work surface or breakfast bar. Some are stylishly studded with tiny, sparkling, low-voltage halogen downlighters, usually fixed, that throw a narrow, bright beam of light just where it is required.

Good lighting, however, does not have to be ultra high-tech and come as an integral part of the kitchen, with a high price tag. Simple fittings can effectively illuminate work areas. A pair of stainless steel clip-on spotlights or a wall-mounted aluminium spot on a concertina arm can look very much a feature in its own right. They are also highly practical, being easy to move with no need to channel into plaster or rewire to fit them. Even department stores and DIY outlets now have a great selection of ideas. Look out for so-called "functional plant uplighters", which can be slipped into a pot of fresh herbs to add texture and mood in the corner of the food preparation area.

Kitchen safety

It is well worth noting a few safety points when lighting your kitchen:

- *Never use a bulb of a higher wattage than that recommended by the fitting*
- *Have old wiring checked by a qualified electrician before installing any new lighting*
- *Never be tempted to overload a transformer*
- *Employ an electrician to install recessed lights to ensure sufficient ceiling space and adequate ventilation; low-voltage halogen units in particular get extremely hot*
- *Take care when angling spotlights over dangerous work areas, such as the hob, to avoid dazzling glare*
- *Never position a light where it is likely to be splashed with water*
- *Do not allow flexes and wiring to trail across work surfaces or the floor*

dining rooms

Whether you are throwing a celebratory party for friends or having a small family get-together, good dining room lighting can help you define the mood of the meal. Part of the pleasure of eating is visual – the colours and presentation of food are as appetizing as the smell – so you will want to see the food you are eating clearly. It is no coincidence that fast-food outlets are bright and well lit; it helps to make the food look good and keeps people moving. Restaurants, on the other hand, are designed with a different objective in mind. Here, the idea is to create a leisurely ambience in which diners can linger and take pleasure in good food and good conversation. There will be times when you want to create both types of setting in your own dining room.

If you are lucky enough to have a separate dining room devoted to entertaining, let a sense of the dramatic take over. The room will most often be used at night, so give your imagination free reign and experiment with theatrical chandeliers, intimate wall lights and romantic candles. Take your cue from restaurants, which are increasingly using lighting systems in a decorative and even sculptural way. Bear in mind that you are trying to create an atmosphere that is instrumental in people enjoying each other's company, so a soft, flattering light is essential. A combination of good ambient lighting with an intimate but directional illumination over the dining table is the accepted formula.

Many contemporary homes do not have a separate dining room. Demands on space, far more relaxed and informal entertaining and an easy-come, easy-go flexible family life, where everyone does their own thing, have all played a role in this. However, a clever lighting scheme can effectively isolate a dining area in an open-plan living space. In a joint kitchen/dining room, you will want to divorce the dining table from the adjacent kitchen, with its utilitarian working surfaces and equipment. Similarly in a dining/sitting room, you will sometimes wish to separate the eating area from the lounging area, so you do not have to look upon the devastation of a just-finished meal when you are relaxing afterwards. The challenge in such a home is to create a cosy and intimate atmosphere within a larger area of bustle, activity and family life.

▼ Large metal pendants operated on dimmer switches can alter from a strong illumination for day to a soft glow by night.

▲ Here, many windows create enough ambient light for daytime dining. By night the elaborate candelabra adds intimacy.

Changes through the day

The dining room is used throughout the day as well as in the evening, so flexibility is a key lighting requirement. In an open-plan kitchen/dining room where the family congregates to eat, the first consideration should be achieving good ambient lighting. With poor natural light – in a basement dining room, for example – all-day artificial lighting may be required. Fit the system with dimmers and incorporate light-reactive switches to ensure you have a flexible lighting scheme that is responsive to changing daylight conditions. The arrangement should also incorporate fittings that can provide a softer tone and level of lighting for the evening.

If you have a through-room that features a kitchen at one end and a dining area at the other, use low-voltage downlighters or spots in the kitchen area and fit them with dimmers. This will produce a clean, white ambient light in the kitchen area, but at the same time provides a good starting point for adjustable ambient lighting in the dining area. From this basis you can add more atmosphere to the dining area with warm tungsten wall lights and table lamps. Low-voltage halogen spots can be trained on paintings and other features of interest.

Conservatory dining

A conservatory is the perfect place to throw summer lunch parties. Creating the atmosphere of *al fresco* dining indoors, with the sun flooding in, is easy if you have large windows that open onto a garden and even better if you can incorporate a glass or transparent roof. The best conservatory designs have floor-to-ceiling French windows on three sides to let in maximum light and warmth, so you will rarely need additional ambient lighting during the day.

To keep the daytime look as light and airy as possible, choose light colours for walls and paintwork. Bear in mind that if the conservatory is south-facing, you may find the natural light too bright. Dazzle and glare are not conducive to a relaxing atmosphere and could even cause headaches. If this becomes a problem, try fitting adjustable Pinoleum roof blinds. A deep cream or sage green colour will screen out the intense sunlight without creating gloominess. Colonial-style shutters or wooden slats are also suitable for conservatory-style settings.

Conversely, if the conservatory faces north and has a solid roof, you may need to enhance the natural ambient light. A large gilt mirror placed high on the solid wall of the conservatory and facing the windows, for instance, will

▼ An electrical candelabra is the perfect choice for this dining room. Use low wattage bulbs and combine with real candles.

▼ Contemporary "bare wire" installlations give a good deal of flexibility. You can move the low voltage halogen fittings at will.

bounce light around the room and illuminate any dark, dingy corners.

Of course, natural light may be appropriate for breakfast on a Sunday morning but it will not be suitable for a formal evening party, so an artificial lighting scheme will be necessary. Consider how and when the dining room will be used and keep the lighting arrangement flexible by fitting dimmers, so the lights can be adjusted with the flick of a switch. At night you may choose to dim the lights or even dispense with them altogether in favour of romantic candlelight. This can be particularly effective in a conservatory with a glass roof – with a very low level of lighting you will be able to see the stars twinkling through the roof. Plan in advance to ensure you have the right type of lighting for every eventuality.

Downlighters and bare-wire installations

For the ultimate in contemporary minimalism, nothing can beat the latest bare-wire installations, with multiple closed dichroic reflectors suspended from them. Not only are these extremely stylish, they also have the advantage that the tiny low-voltage lights can be moved freely along the wire to wherever they are required. Fit a dimmer so that you can adjust the lighting level, from clear, bright light without shadows for daytime dining to a softer, serene light for the evenings.

Positioning is all-important with downlighters but, with this free-track arrangement, you can even remove the reflectors altogether if you wish to alter the layout of the

▼ Suspended between two "bare wires", this low voltage fitting can be moved freely up and down to give ultimate flexibility.

▼ This traditional chandelier is actually a modern reproduction. If you buy a genuine, old fitting, get it checked by an electrician.

▶ In an elegant, spacious dining room, two chandeliers are better than one. Always make sure they are fixed to load-bearing joists.

dining area – for a big party, for instance. In general, however, downlighters should be sited so that they illuminate the table. They can be staggered at different heights to create a modern effect, but do not place them directly over the heads of the diners because this will cast unattractive shadows over their faces.

Although the arrangement is flexible along the length of the wires, it is fixed in the horizontal plane, so you will be limited as to where you can move the dining table once the scheme is finalized.

Chandelier magic

A favourite choice for lighting a dining room is a chandelier, which adds a touch of the dramatic to any dining room, particularly if positioned above the table. During the daytime, sunlight glancing off a crystal chandelier lends a room elegance and charm. At night, nothing can compete with the glamour of a sparkling chandelier, whether lit with real candles or candle-style tungsten bulbs. A chandelier is undoubtedly the ultimate in romantic dining.

Chandeliers come in many shapes and sizes, from the simplest wrought-iron designs to splendidly ornate affairs

with hundreds of coloured glass droplets. Some take candles, others are electric; the choice is endless. If you decide you want candles for some occasions and electric light for others, adaptors are available from specialist lighting stores that enable you to switch from one form of chandelier to another. These comprise an integral socket and hook that you wire into the ceiling. The electrical chandelier is fitted with a plug that is inserted into the ceiling socket to complete the circuit. When you wish to use a candle chandelier, simply unplug and unhook the electrical one. You can then insert a matching, but unwired, connector into the socket and hang your candle chandelier in place.

Candles or electric?

There is nothing quite like candlelight for creating an intimate atmosphere. However, even an eight- to ten-candle chandelier will not emit a huge amount of light, particularly in a large room. If you choose a candle chandelier, therefore, you will have to supplement the level of illumination with additional forms of electrical lighting.

A note of caution: large numbers of lit candles create a lot of heat, so make sure the chandelier is hung sufficiently

▼ An alternative way of hanging a pendant lamp is in a group of three and at staggered heights above a table, as shown here.

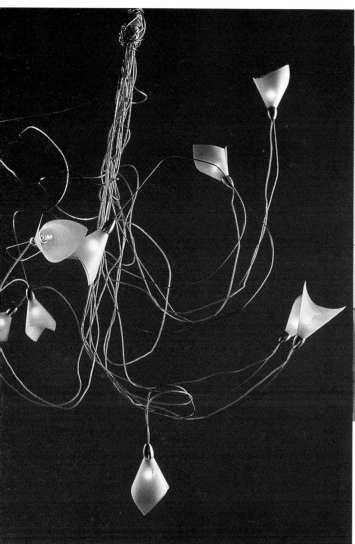

▲ This modern interpretation of a chandelier features multiple low voltage capsules with tiny acrylic collars.

low to avoid marking the ceiling with soot. This could even constitute a fire risk, so take extra care and never leave lit candles unattended.

Electric chandeliers are much more versatile than their candle counterparts. Some can be fitted with low-wattage tungsten bulbs to create a cosy background lighting; others feature multiple low-voltage halogen capsules that throw out minute sparkles of intense white light to twinkle against the crystal droplets. State-of-the-art designs include Medusa-style chandeliers of twisting, curling tubes of metal, each concluding in a tiny, pinpoint halogen capsule. The effect is striking.

For traditionalists, second-hand electric chandeliers are readily available and, if you are prepared to do a little work, can be reasonably priced. To restore and update a classic design, replace any missing crystal parts and paint over the gilt with metallic silver paint. Antique shops often have remnant boxes of chandelier components. They can be cleaned by dissolving a couple of denture cleaning tablets in some water and leaving the chandelier pieces to soak for a couple of hours. This is an excellent way to bring dirty glass or crystal back to life.

To add a touch of colour to your chandelier, attach coloured rather than clear glass droplets with picture wire. Have some fun by mixing and matching shades. Existing clear glass can also be painted using artists' glass paint. The result will be a sparkling focal point that will draw attention to the dining table, making it the centrepiece of the whole room.

Cleaning a crystal chandelier can be difficult, but there are many special sprays that will do the job without your having to dismantle the whole thing or call in professional help. Protect the floor beneath the fitting, then spray the chandelier liberally from the top downwards at a distance of around 15cm (6in). Rub gently with a soft cloth to remove ingrained dirt.

A word of warning: chandeliers are composed of a strong, metal-based frame and lots of glass, so they are

▼ Open metal shades look good, but can dazzle. Make sure you hang them sufficiently low over your dining table to avoid this.

▲ Look out for fittings which feature mutliple integral pendants with coloured mini shades. They make a strong style statement.

extremely heavy. Always make sure that they are secured firmly to a load-bearing beam and not just in the ceiling plaster. Seek professional help if in doubt.

The table as centrepiece

The centrepiece of any dining room is the dining table. A good lighting scheme will enhance the table as the focal point of the room as well as create the best overall illumination. A large, ornate overhead chandelier is the perfect choice for a traditional round table; a long, rectangular table that seats many people in a line, however, cries out for something more imaginative.

A line of modern pendant lights is a practical option that will light the whole table. These should be suspended low enough not to dazzle the diners or cause any glare, while still illuminating the table thoroughly. Nowadays, designers frequently mix and match three or more different, but complimentary, styles of shade. This is the same principle as mixing and matching other items that were traditionally bought in sets – china and dining chairs, for example – and mix-and-match lighting is simply an extension of this idea. Odd sets help to create an informal mood that is synonymous with contemporary living.

Another quirky idea is to hang the shades at different heights over the table, to give the lighting an attractive architectural appeal as well as illuminating the table area. This design device is easy to achieve and looks very stylish.

Choosing pendant shades

When choosing shades, bear in mind that the wider the shade, the greater the area over which the light will fall.

▼ In this traditional setting, a side table of decanters and glasses looks elegant in the warmth of tungsten lamp light.

Even if you choose a very wide shade, however, you will still need at least two pendants to illuminate a long dining table adequately. The drawback with open pendant shades is that they can cause dazzle if suspended too high. To avoid this problem, fit your lights with low-wattage bulbs; 40-watt bulbs should be adequate as long as there are two or more pendants.

Long, narrow shades with the bulb well recessed within them will create a cosier atmosphere, especially if they are suspended low over the dining table. However, several of these will be required to create sufficient ambient light, particularly if they are opaque shades. These do not allow much light to be thrown out horizontally and, in effect, are more like wide spotlights over the table.

▼ Fitted shelving and storage units are perfect for fitting recessed downlighters. Use them to highlight accessories and glassware.

▲ This modern light features a red polypropylene shade that gives out a warm, glowing light – perfect for the dining room.

Small, coloured glass shades are another possibility and, in soft tones of blue and pale green, can be a stylish option. Fit them with halogen bulbs, which throw out a clear, bright white light that will not distort the colour of the shades.

If you want something to cast a greater spread of ambient light – such as that required for everyday family meals – choose ribbed glass shades. These look stylishly modern; light shines through them as if through a prism, breaking the light up and scattering it diffusely throughout the room. This effect can be further enhanced by using pearl tungsten bulbs rather than clear ones. Crown-silvered bulbs are another good idea; they reflect light back into the shade, diffusing it and reducing glare.

Lighting side tables and shelving

Away from the main table, there are further decisions to be made in terms of decorative and accent lighting. Side tables, consoles, storage units and open shelving all provide opportunities both to add to the ambient light and to highlight other features in the room. Ideally, these secondary forms of lighting should not create too great a contrast or take the focus away from the dining table.

A tall, small-shaded lamp is a traditional feature on a sideboard and can be an excellent way to add atmosphere to the dining room while illuminating a drinks tray, cutlery or china. Most of the light will be directed downwards but some will be thrown up to add to the intimacy of the atmosphere. The darker the shade, the more dramatic the effect. Place a pair of lamps at either end of a side table to create an impressive, formal effect. Fit the lamps with 40-watt bulbs, or an even lower wattage, to ensure the lighting is soft, warm and not overpowering.

▲ This shelf unit looks quite different when lit with different lights. Here four uplights wash the unit from the front.

▲ The same set of shelves look very dramatic when lit with single downlights at the sides and lateral lighting in the central area.

This device is not limited to traditional settings. In an open-plan dining area, lamps are a good way to delineate the dining furniture from a nearby kitchen or sitting room. An ultra-modern lamp with a red polypropylene shade will give out an intense red glow that draws your attention while at the same time producing a modest amount of cosy ambient light. This kind of lamp will resemble an illuminated sculpture if placed on a sideboard. A matching pair of lamps can be used for extra impact.

Modern storage units with integral low-voltage downlighters ensure that stored items can be selected easily. They can be left switched on throughout a meal to add to the level of ambient light. To illuminate open shelving, bookcases or a corner drinks cupboard, two or three directable low-voltage spots are a practical arrangement. Remember that spots and downlighters are more flexible if fitted with dimmers, which means you can make subtle adjustments to atmosphere and mood throughout the day and night. Combine them with tungsten uplighters trained on pictures and decorative wall lights to illuminate any dark corners; all these forms of lighting will enhance points of interest in the room without detracting from the main focus – the dining table.

Having a party

A good dining room lighting scheme is invaluable when entertaining. As well as creating the right atmosphere for your party – from cosy and intimate to bright and cheerful, for example – it is important that the lighting in the dining room is also flattering to the complexion, helps to put your dinner guests at ease and makes food look even more appetizing. Tungsten is the best choice of bulb for this. However, candles give out an even warmer yellow glow than tungsten and are the most intimate and flattering light of all. There is a place for candles in even the most mundane dining area.

Apart from chandeliers, a party atmosphere can be enhanced by putting a tiny nightlight in a coloured glass votive next to each place setting. Consider creating a centrepiece of floating candles and heavily scented flowers in a large, low bowl – it will imbue the party with an enchanting light and will not act as a barrier between the diners in the way that many more elaborate, taller flower arrangements can do.

If you want to place candlesticks on the dining table, choose tall, thin ones. These are less likely to obstruct the view of the person opposite than large, grand candlesticks,

▲ Midnight blue walls set the scene for an intimate party. The fairy lights, table candles and wall lanterns add to the mood.

which are best positioned out of the way on side tables. In a conservatory setting, citronella candles will ward off summer insects as well as scent the evening air. To set the ultimate party scene, however, you can rely on twinkling sets of fairy lights plugged into a nearby socket and entwined around a pair of fig or bay trees. All you have to do then is dim the lights and enjoy.

◄ Tiny blue glass votives combine with white hyacinths and candles to create soft lighting and a heady, scented atmosphere.

bedrooms

Bedrooms, in particular, require a sympathetic lighting treatment. Bedroom lighting should be bright, invigorating and agreeable to wake up to, yet calm, soothing and easy to relax in. Achieving these contrasting effects will require a combination of several different types of lighting.

In addition to sleeping, there are many leisure activities that you will want to enjoy in the bedroom – reading a good book, listening to music, watching television and sharing intimate moments with your partner, to name but a few – and each of these activities demands a different lighting effect, from a task light for reading to the atmospheric lighting that makes listening to music so much more enjoyable.

We spend a third of our lives sleeping and many more hours in the bedroom before and after going to sleep. This is the most personal room in the home, where you begin and end each day, so it should reflect your personality and aspirations. In fact, these crucial aspects of your life will be affected by the quality of your bedroom surroundings, of which lighting plays a vital part.

Sad, then, that so many bedrooms are neglected when it comes to lighting. A common bedroom lighting design consists of a central pendant fitting and a pair of bedside lamps. Yet here, more than in any other room in the home, the lighting scheme should be infinitely adjustable and flexible, so that you can adapt it to suit both day and night, whatever the season and whatever your needs and mood may be.

A single overhead fitting will create an unsympathetic quality of light. When you consider that you spend a substantial amount of time lying in bed, the idea of looking up at a glaring light source is most unsatisfactory. Generally, it is better to rely on a combination of lamps and wall fittings to create an acceptable level of background lighting. Uplighting is also practical in the bedroom, since it throws light up to the ceiling while concealing the light source. The reflected light creates a softer, more diffuse effect – just what is needed to create a relaxing bedroom ambience. Finally, it is important to fit dimmers to each lighting system to achieve maximum flexibility.

▼ Nothing beats natural sunlight in the mornings. Consider enlarging or adding more windows to your room.

▲ The airy appeal of this bedroom is due to the white walls and ceilings. Extra light is "borrowed" from the area behind the bed.

More natural daylight

There is nothing quite like waking up early on a summer's morning to the warm glow of the dawn sunlight. So much the better if you have large French doors opening onto a balcony or garden. If not, consider increasing the amount of natural daylight that enters your bedroom by installing roof lights. These draw the eye outwards and create a feeling of spaciousness, dappling the room with the promise of a sunny day ahead.

Another option is to increase the size of the window. The easiest way to do this is to remove the area of wall below the window and lower the sill. There are no structural implications and it only requires basic building skills. To take things a step further, you can increase the window area by widening the opening all round, but for this you will need to consult a qualified builder. If you want to convert a sash window into French doors, ask a builder to install a load-bearing beam across the top of the window opening. This is also necessary if you wish to insert a new window into a solid wall.

If you can, position the new window on the opposite wall to the existing one. This improves the quality of the ambient light by reducing dazzle and shadow, while at the same time increasing the diversity and level of light throughout the day. An easier option is to replace some of the traditional bricks in the wall with glass ones. This introduces extra light into the room but with fewer problems, as the glass bricks are to some extent load-bearing in themselves, unlike a window pane. However, always check with a builder or an architect first.

Internal windows or open room dividers can also improve the level of background lighting. Replace solid doors with opaque glass doors or insert long, narrow sheets of glass into the existing doors just below ceiling height to "borrow" light from an adjacent room.

Pale pastel or all-white walls and bed linen can also help to improve the quality of limited ambient light. Remember that dark colours tend to absorb rather than reflect light and can produce a claustrophobic feeling. Ceilings and floors act as giant reflectors, so keep them as light as possible and install low-voltage spotlights and downlighters to maximize the amount of illumination. Avoid using these fittings directly over the bed, however, as they will cause too much glare. Also bear in mind that matt or textured surfaces absorb light, while shiny surfaces such as mirrors make the most of it.

▲ This bedroom has a five-star hotel feeling due to the elegant wall lights over the bed, enhanced by neat halogen downlighters.

Ambient lighting

Ambient light should form the main source of illumination in the bedroom. It should produce a neutral and relaxing background, which can then be enhanced by other forms of lighting, such as bedside lights, accent and decorative lights. It is important that the ambient light is dimmable. You need to be able to adjust the level of lighting in the bedroom subtly, so that you can create any type of atmosphere you wish as well as meet various practical considerations – for instance, the level of light required at night will by no means be sufficient during the day.

A traditional bedroom lighting design could start with an overhead chandelier fitted with clear, twinkling bulbs. These should not be too bright – they should add to the romance of the room rather than dazzle the eyes. To this you might add a pair of bedside lamps fitted with opaque shades, so that the light is thrown both up the walls and down onto the bedside table. Halogen lighting concealed behind cornicing that is just below ceiling height is another good device for creating ambient light without glare. By increasing or decreasing the intensity of these lighting systems using dimmers, a whole variety of lighting effects

▼ Dark walls demand good lighting. Here the room benefits from strong natural light and a quality Anglepoise task light.

is possible – you can create a warm, cosy ambience for settling down in bed with a good book, or a seductive glow for snuggling down with your partner.

Remember that the level of background light will be affected by the depth of colour you choose for the walls and soft furnishings of your bedroom. With deep red walls,

for instance, you need good daylight as well as bright artificial lighting to compensate for the dark colour. Low-voltage halogen lighting is probably the best choice to brighten and whiten the effect, rather than tungsten, which is too yellow. Add white bed linen and drapes to brighten the look even further.

▼ This potentially gloomy loft room gets an all-white treatment bar one orange wall. The wall lights are left permanently on.

For a bedroom situated in the eaves, achieving good ambient lighting can be difficult, as the source of natural light is often a single small window. Make the most of this by keeping the window treatment minimal – a simple roller blind is a good idea. Choose a dark fabric so you can sleep at night. Paint the walls white to reflect as much of the available light around the room as possible, then add atmosphere with brightly coloured soft furnishings and perhaps paint one wall with a similar shade, to warm the overall effect. One way to light the room well is to keep a pair of wall lights high above the bed permanently lit; use tungsten bulbs to give a natural sunshine effect.

▼ This candlestick lamp has a slim base which leaves plenty of room on the bedside table for books and a cup of coffee.

▼ A beaded shade diffuses the light to create a soft. moody quality that is perfect for the bedroom.

Bedside lamps

As well as ambient lighting, more direct lighting is required on either side of the bed. Many people read in bed before going to sleep, so good task lighting is important. Place a light at each side of the bed; they should have separate controls for those times when one partner wants to go straight to sleep and the other does not. A typical approach is to place a pair of tungsten table lamps on bedside tables, which emit a cosy light.

There are several things to bear in mind when making your selection from the huge number of bedside lamps available in lighting stores. The height of the lamp is important, since it determines where the light will fall. If the lamp is too short, it will illuminate the table beneath it with a small pool of light and throw out the rest above the shade as ambient light. This is unsatisfactory, because you need most of the light to fall on the pages of your book – without disturbing your sleeping partner. Choose a lamp that is at least 20cm (8in) tall, so that the shade is well above your book. In addition, make sure the light can be operated and controlled without your having to get out of bed. If your bedside table is fairly small, choose a lamp with a narrow base to leave room on the table for other

objects. Candlestick lamps are a popular choice, since they give the necessary height but without width.

Choosing a shade

The shade should be in proportion to the lamp base for aesthetic reasons, but remember that the wider the shade, the bigger the pool of light. Choose a shade that is narrow enough to cast the majority of the light onto the pages of your book, but not onto the pillow where it could shine into your eyes and dazzle you.

If you do not want to disturb your partner, opaque shades are a practical choice. With these the light is directed down and across your reading matter rather than thrown out into the room. If you choose a black shiny shade with a gold liner, this will have a similar effect. However, bear in mind that the gold lining will make the light very warm and yellow, which may cause eyestrain if it is not bright enough to read by. You could insert a higher wattage bulb, but check first that the shade is designed to take it or there could be a fire risk. A clear tungsten bulb creates a harder light, while a pearl-finish one diffuses the light away from the filament and therefore casts much softer shadows.

▼ This metal shade is pierced with tiny holes to allow the light to shine through like twinkling stars.

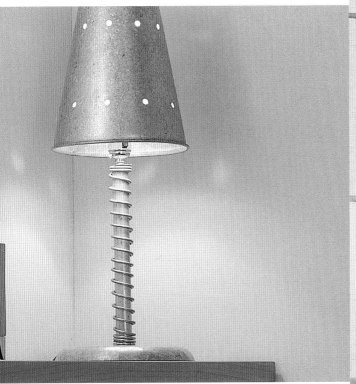

▲ Modern lamp styles feature cylindrical, brushed metal bases with simple, unadorned white shades.

Metal shades can be extremely decorative, particularly those that have holes cut or punched into them. This allows the tungsten light to shine through and create delicate star-like patterns that are wonderfully mood enhancing. Other shades that particularly lend themselves to bedside lighting are beaded ones. Whether you use these shades with candles or tungsten bulbs (both types of fitting are available), they create a lovely boudoir effect – the light is dappled with jewel tones, depending on the colour of the beading. Shades with beads hanging down from the edge are especially attractive, creating an intimate, sensuous atmosphere.

In a bedroom that is situated in the eaves of the house, exploit this architectural configuration by fitting sheet mirror onto the angled part of the wall, beside the bed. By placing your bedside lamp in front of the mirror, you can effectively double the intensity of the light from that one source.

Dimmable fittings on the bedside lamps make it easy to adjust the level of light, at the flick of a switch, to suit your requirements. Make sure the dimmers are accessible from the bed and are on different circuits for each lamp, so you can vary the levels of light for each one independently.

Flexible bedside lighting

If you want something more contemporary than traditional table lamps, there are a number of modern variations in the form of low-voltage halogen designs. Flexibility is the name of the game here. Fittings include pivoting, angled, swinging and extendible heads, as well as bendy Anglepoises. As you shift your position in bed to achieve maximum comfort, you need to be able to redirect your bedside lighting accordingly. In a small bedroom, where there simply is not enough room for bedside tables, a good alternative is to use wall-mounted swing-arm lamps. Apart from saving dramatically on floor space, these have the advantage of being a highly flexible source of illumination, so that you can target the light where you need it.

▼ Correct positioning of fixed bedside wall lights is essential to ensure there is no glare, yet there is enough light to read by.

▼ Fixed, overhead wall lights, plus a pair of bedside lamps ensures ultimate flexibility in this smart bedroom.

The positioning of these lamps is crucial. A foolproof way to figure out at what height to position the light is to lie on the bed and settle down into your most comfortable reading position. Then ask someone to measure from the floor to just above your shoulder height. This is the optimum spot to place the task lighting, so it shines between your head and your reading matter. It is generally around 80–90cm (32–36in) above the mattress and directly overhead. You will want to mount the wall lights at the same height on both sides of the bed for aesthetic reasons, so you and your partner may have to compromise.

Always check how far the arm of the lamp will extend before purchasing it, because this determines how manoeuvrable the light will be once mounted. Before screwing your lamps to the wall, check that they have the full range that you require.

If you would like wall-mounted lamps but do not want the expense of channelling electrical cables into the wall, buy fittings that are designed to be hung from a nail or screw, with a cable that can be plugged into a nearby socket. Choose a design that has a switch fitted into the cable near the light source, so the lamp can be switched on and off from the bed. For maximum flexibility, there are snake-like, bendable metal fittings that look chic and up-to-the-minute, and which deliver a narrow beam of halogen light just where you want it.

Alternatively, you may prefer to purchase a neat, floor-standing lamp with a pivoting head that you can angle over your reading matter. If so, always position the base well away from where you put your feet when getting out of bed or you may tip it over. To avoid this problem, look for a light source that you can clip onto your bedhead. Choose a light with the capsule recessed into the shade so that it does not dazzle your eyes when you look up.

▼ Some task lights can be simply screwed to the wall, rather than chanelled into the plaster. Less expensive, yet still effective.

Dressing areas

The bedroom is the room where we dress and prepare for the day ahead. You need bright lighting for these activities and, in particular, light with true colour rendering, so you can judge your appearance accurately before you face the world. Fixed overhead lighting arrangements are the norm in most bedrooms, notably pendants, but these can create quite the wrong type of lighting for dressing and makeup purposes – one that causes shadows and intense illumination in all the wrong places. To use a pendant to best effect, look for an enclosed silk shade in a deep colour, which will throw out a soft, warm light at night that infuses the ambient light with a tinge of colour.

For daytime the ideal solution is good natural light, but you will also need good-quality artificial illumination, probably created with low-voltage halogen. This is particularly important in the winter, when most of us get up and prepare for the day in the dark.

▼ These "snake head" lights are neat and unobtrusive yet give a clear directable light for reading in bed.

▲ Good lighting is essential in a dressing area. Natural daylight will give true colour rendering; ideal for applying make-up.

The best position for a long mirror is where you can view yourself in good natural light. Place it in front of a large window so that the daylight falls over you evenly from head to toe. Do not position the mirror sideways to the window or the light will only illuminate one side of you, throwing your far side into shadow.

Lighting mirrors

Wall mirrors that are lit from directly above will cast a deep shadow over your lower half. Ideally, you need to have a light source at both sides of the mirror so that you get an even flood of light from side to side. The light should also, if possible, illuminate the whole mirror from top to bottom. You can achieve this with a set of low-voltage halogen spots set into a false wall and evenly spaced on either side of the mirror. You can then adjust the direction of the lighting to give perfect illumination without glare.

A series of ceiling downlighters can look too utilitarian in a bedroom setting and will cast discrete pools of light. These may be perfect for illuminating a work surface but they are not suitable for dressing by. Being lit from overhead in this way will also cause glare, which could disturb a sleeping partner.

Some built-in closets have a set of small, low-voltage halogen lights recessed into prominent mouldings just above mirrored doors, which give excellent light. Look for eyeball spots that you can adjust, as fixed lights can be too harsh. Have this circuit fitted to a dimmer control so that you can adjust the level of illumination to suit your needs – for example, to enhance the ambient light when you want to create a softer, more intimate mood.

Alternatively, by recessing new-generation fluorescent strips into a false wall behind a panel of opaque glass, you can flood the area in front of the mirror with bright yet diffuse light. This means no shadowing, perfect for checking your appearance.

A pair of floor-standing lights may also suffice, but they should have a wide, light-emitting surface, such as a cream shade, to give good ambient light. The drawback with floor-standing lighting is that it tends to illuminate your upper half far better than your lower half, but you may feel this is not a problem. Tungsten bulbs give a warm, flattering effect but they can alter the appearance of colours and skin tone.

If the light source is situated behind you – that is, you are "backlit" – this will create a highly flattering image.

▼ Position your dressing table mirror near to good daylight. At night the light source should also come from both sides.

▼ This series of pendants creates a high quality ambient light for selecting clothes from the bank of wardrobes.

◄ Some modern wardrobes feature integral lighting, such as this state-of-the-art unit with fixed halogen downlighters.

However, you will not be able to see yourself as others will see you for the rest of the day, so it is much better to opt for lighting that is truthful. You can then amend your appearance as necessary.

Avoid placing lights where they will shine straight at the mirror, since these will cause a dazzling glare that is neither aesthetically appealing nor practical. The same rules apply to dressing table mirrors as to wall mirrors. A pair of table lamps or wall lights, positioned either side of the dressing table, with the mirror at the centre, provides the best illumination.

Lighting wardrobes

Make sure that cupboards, wardrobes and closets are well lit on the inside, for selecting and replacing clothes. Light built-in wardrobes with neat, low-voltage halogen bulbs that give good colour rendering and are small enough to be recessed into the ceiling of the wardrobe. However, even mini-fluorescent strips will be an improvement, although they can taint the colour of clothes with a slightly unearthly shade. Both types of fitting can be installed so that the light automatically comes on when the door is opened, rather like a refrigerator light.

▲ A collection of scented candles will add wafts of perfume and a romantic mood to your bedroom.

▲ In this masculine bedroom navy walls and dark furniture are warmed by a number of traditional, glowing tungsten lamps.

Adding atmosphere

Bedrooms should be romantic as well as practical, and there is nothing more Byronic than lamplight, either in the form of chandeliers or candles. Put candles in wall sconces, group them in coloured glass jars or place them in candelabra – the warm, flickering light of a burning candle is immensely appealing. You will, of course, need a great number of candles to create enough illumination to light a bedroom adequately, so you will probably wish to combine them with other forms of ambient light. A log fire is spectacular if you are lucky enough to have an open fireplace in your bedroom and it will create a wonderful atmosphere on a winter evening.

If not, there are other ways to create an intimate mood in your bedroom. Try painting two of your walls a deep midnight blue and the other two walls pure white. This might sound a little odd but the effect is truly wonderful. The white walls make the most of the light and are a crisp, clean antidote to gloom, while the navy creates a midnight backdrop for candles and lamplight. Use cream, pleated shades that will glow warmly when illuminated by tungsten lighting. Finally, make the most of a pendant fitting by hanging an enclosed crystal lantern or chandelier

from it. Fit this with low-powered bulbs that will twinkle softly in the background.

To get as much power as you can from wall sconces, look for designs with a sheet of reflective metal or a mirror behind them, which will double the level of illumination. You can create the same effect, even in a contemporary setting, by placing a modern wall light or wall sconce in front of a large sheet of mirror, perhaps in an alcove.

When using candles, reduce the level of background lighting with dimmers to a gentle all-over yellow glow, so the real flames are the main focus. A soft ambient lighting is the best foil for kinetic lighting. Even these days, clever use of candles can be a practical way to supplement the overall level of lighting without the need to channel electrical cables into plaster walls. They are particularly appropriate to the bedroom, the most seductive room in the home. Combine scented candles with soft music and you can delight three of your senses at once.

Lighting children's rooms

Children's bedrooms have a different set of criteria when it comes to lighting than adults' bedrooms – children often play, read and socially interact in their bedrooms and each

▲ This child's loft bedroom gets plenty of light from a pair of skylights, tungsten spotlights and a small coloured lamp.

of these activities requires different lighting. Children may also be afraid of the dark, so you need to take this into account by introducing some sympathetic background lighting that you can leave on all night. With small babies that require feeding in the early hours, choose low-level, soft task lighting, such as a tungsten lamp.

Consider fitting extra sockets, using different bulb intensities and installing free-form track lighting to increase flexibility. As your child grows up, the lighting should be adaptable enough to accommodate his or her developing

needs. It is vital, however, to bear safety in mind – ensure that the sockets are covered and that hot light fittings, switches, flexes and cables are out of reach.

Free-standing light fittings are all too easy for a curious toddler to pull over, so fixed lighting is your best option in a child's bedroom, either mounted on the walls or recessed into the ceiling. Low-voltage halogen spots are a practical choice. Fit them with dimmers to provide the flexibility you need for dealing with everything from night feeds to children who fear the dark.

studies

More people now work from home than ever before. By the year 2020 statisticians predict that one in five of us will be a homeworker. Technology is developing at such an extraordinary rate that we can now manage our lives from our own homes at the touch of a keypad, from buying a book to checking our bank balance. As this trend develops, slowly but surely the study is gaining greater prominence within the home.

The study, or workroom, can vary from a bedroom office to a basement workshop, from somewhere to read a book to a place for practicing a musical instrument or using a sewing machine. All workrooms have to cater for specific activities and these are as many and diverse as the people who do them. Similarly, each activity has different lighting demands, which need to be met if the room is to function efficiently. You will need good light by which to perform close-up work, often at a computer screen, but you will also want to create a warm ambience – the room should be welcoming and comfortable to work in, though not too relaxing!

The influence of the environment on our sense of well-being and our ability to perform efficiently is well documented. Unfortunately, many people have to work in poorly arranged, drab offices, lit by antiquated and flickering fluorescent strip lights. In your own home, however, you have the opportunity to design your workspace just as you want it.

As with other rooms in the home, the ambient lighting should be your starting point. This can sometimes be difficult to get right in a study, which is often relegated to a small room at the back of the house, perhaps lacking in natural daylight. If you go out to work all day and generally use the workroom in the evening, you will certainly need some good-quality artificial lighting.

Another consideration is space. It may be that you cannot devote a whole room to being a full-time study – your workroom may also act as a spare bedroom, be part of an open-plan living area or a corner of the dining room. In such cases you will have to compromise on how your work area is designed and lit, but any problems are easily surmountable if you keep your lighting scheme flexible.

▼ Windows positioned high in the wall give this workroom a good ambient light without dazzling the desk area.

▲ A floor-to-ceiling plate glass window creates a wonderful wall of light. White paper blinds are perfect at softening the effect.

▼ Never work with your computer screen facing a window, instead place it beside or beneath the adjacent window.

Working windows

Privacy is not usually a problem in workrooms, so if light is limited, leave windows unencumbered by curtains. Good natural light, however, can actually be a drawback if you work at a computer, since it can cause reflections and glare off the screen. The problem can be eased by reducing the amount of ambient light that enters the room through the windows, but it is important that the room does not become a gloomy, depressing environment. The best solution lies in the appropriate orientation of the desk and computer screen in relation to the windows.

The optimum arrangement is to position your computer screen at right angles to a nearby window. If you have a high window, it is a good idea to place your desk beneath and just to one side of it for good ambient lighting without glare. Try not to sit at the computer with your back to the window – you will see a bright reflection of the window in your screen, which can make working almost impossible as well as lead to eyestrain. If you have no choice, you can buy a special filter that fits over the screen to minimize glare.

In a very small study where you have limited options, invest in a dark roller blind that you can adjust up and

▲ If your workroom lacks natural light, you can "borrow" it from an adjoining room. Strips of glass bricks are an attractive device.

down depending on your light requirements. Venetian blinds are even more versatile. Choose the sort that are perforated with tiny pinholes; this allows some of the ambient light through but without uncomfortable glare.

If you are starting from scratch or having your workroom specially built as an extension, glass bricks are a useful way to diffuse natural daylight. A double row of glass bricks set into a wall will add ambient light just where you need it. Also consider installing sliding doors, leading to an adjacent hallway or another room. These can be used both to regulate the level of light and to provide instant privacy when you need to make an important call.

▼ Be imaginative with your lighting solutions. Here the cabling for spotlights has been recessed into a decorative wooden panel.

▲ This dining room-cum-study is lit by a pair of modern aluminium pendants with a task light for close-up desk work.

Artificial ambient light

If the level of daylight in your study is poor – in a basement workroom, for example – or you find that the ambient light is dramatically reduced by your need to shield your computer screen, the room will benefit from additional daytime lighting. A row of eyeball spots trained high on a white wall will produce a diffuse light that is also flexible (by simply realigning the spots). This arrangement produces a level of illumination that is both comfortable and good enough to read by. It would be the perfect configuration in a music room, for instance, where you may want to create an intimate mood yet need enough illumination by which to read or write music.

Fixed downlighters should be avoided, because they create intense, dazzling pools of light. In contrast, lights concealed by wooden or metal baffling just below ceiling height offer exactly the sort of diffuse background lighting that is required in a study. They also enhance the effect of a task light used to highlight the desk top.

Pendant lighting

If you study at a dining table, low pendant lights set immediately above the table will illuminate your work area with good-quality lighting. Look for narrow shades, which will cast a defined stream of light exactly where you want it. Choose deep, opaque shades in which the bulb is well recessed to avoid any direct glare. Contemporary metal designs are a stylish and practical option. Use tungsten bulbs for a warm, cosy effect or halogen fittings for a clear, white light that has good colour rendering properties.

Task lighting

Task lights help to concentrate the mind and block out external distractions by focusing a strong beam of light directly onto your work surface. In general, task lighting comprises reading and desk lamps. At its most basic, a task light can be a classic candlestick table lamp with a white shade, which will produce a warm pool of light that is adequate for reading or writing by for short periods. The latest designs, however, generally produce a strong, narrow beam of light that can be directed onto a discreet area of your work surface. To perform effectively, task lights must be directional and concentrated, so that very little of the light spills onto the surrounding area. It is also important that they are adjustable, so that you can alter their position as required.

▲ The smallest alcove can accomodate a desk. Select lighting in keeping with the setting, like this pretty candlestick lamp.

▲ Modern task lights feature futuristic twisting metal arms and halogen capsules (left), but contemporary classic are still very popular, such as this one modelled on the 1950s Bestlite (right).

Traditional task lights

Everyone recognizes the old-fashioned banker's lamp from a thousand old movies. With its curved, green glass shade and brass base, the banker's lamp throws a wide band of light down onto the work surface with no risk of glare. The green glass tints the light with a cool and calming colour that is highly conducive to detailed, concentrated work, without any risk of eyestrain. More contemporary versions feature blue glass with a chrome base, but the principle and quality of light is the same as in the original version.

Other traditional designs include so-called "tole" lights. These have metal shades that direct all the light up or down, thus avoiding glare; in reality, however, they are more decorative than functional.

Good-quality desk lights are available in many classic designs. Still in production is the Bestlite, originally designed in 1950 by Best and Lloyd, with its elegant simplicity, practical curved neck and metal shade. Also look out for the Tango desk lamp, made by Arteluce and designed by S Copeland; it features a limb-like arm and matt black, hooded head and functions like a conventional adjustable table lamp. There is also the TA table light, designed by Peter Nelson. Dating from the 1960s, it has a sleek, matt aluminium shade that moves up and down a narrow metal pole, offering good height and head adjustability. Finally, watch for the Jielde work lamp, a French bench light that can be clamped to a shelf or work surface. It comprises no less than three joints along the main arm, making it highly flexible.

The Anglepoise

The all-time classic desk lamp design is the Anglepoise, which derives its name from its elegant flexibility. Designed in 1934 by George Carwardine, a British car engineer, the Anglepoise has stood the test of time admirably. The lamp comprises a jointed arm held precisely in position by a strong spring, which provides both flexibility and stability. The metal shade itself can also be angled and swivelled to provide even greater flexibility, the key characteristic of a successful task light. Finally, the length of the arm means the base of the lamp can be positioned well away from the work area. Alternatively, space-saving clip-on designs are available that can be clamped to the edge of a desk or to nearby shelving.

Contemporary task lights

The new generation of task lights are far more functional and high-tech in appearance than their traditional counterparts. Some are designed to take halogen reflectors, while others work from fluorescent tubes or tungsten bulbs.

▼ Keep it simple with a spacious, plain desk, a large mirror to make the most of natural daylight and a low voltage task light.

▲ The scene is set for an intimate library atmosphere with these deep blue painted bookshelves and clip-on Anglepoise task lights.

Most offer a high degree of flexibility, with designs that feature jointed or bendable arms and manoeuvrable or twisting heads that can be swivelled in almost any direction. Other models have cantilevered arms with a built-in weight for balancing a fixed head. Look out also for neat, telescopic designs. To avoid being overwhelmed by the choice, first assess how and when you will use the lamp and then judge the merits of each design.

Tungsten or halogen?

Lamps that use low-voltage halogen bulbs are appropriate if you need a narrow, strong beam of light with good colour rendering. This will certainly be the case if you are working on illustrations, fabric designs or looking at colour swatches where you need to see the colours in their true shade. Tungsten bulbs, which cast a yellowish tinge over everything, are not appropriate in such situations. For conventional mains-voltage light fittings, look instead for

◄ Low voltage task lights offer stylish, compact, modern designs with a concentrated source of bright, white light to work by.

▲ An adjustable, floor-standing task light is the perfect solution if you do not want to clutter up your work surface

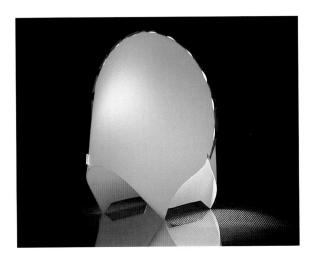

mains-voltage halogen bulbs, which produce a clear, white light. They have a longer life than tungsten and the bulbs will not blacken over time. Alternatively, purchase day-simulation tungsten bulbs, which are clear blue and produce a whiter light than standard tungsten for truer colour rendering. Such "daylight" bulbs are readily available at artist's supply shops.

One drawback with low-voltage halogen task lights is that they need a transformer to convert from mains voltage to the lower voltage at which they operate. This bulky box of tricks is often fitted at the plug or, more often these days, as an integral part of the lamp base. The choice is yours and your decision will largely depend on where you need to save space. Having the transformer as part of the plug means that it will project a little way from the wall socket and you may have to allow for this when positioning your desk, for instance. If the transformer is part of the lamp base, it may take up more space on your desk top, although it does give the lamp excellent stability.

Floor-standing task lights

Another way to avoid having your work surface taken up with large lamp bases is to select a floor-standing task light. These are virtually identical to desk lamps but they stand on the floor and can be positioned next to your desk. Generally, they should be placed on the right if you are right-handed and on the left if you are left-handed. Make sure the neck of the lamp can be extended to reach over your work area and that the lamp is fully adjustable to offer as much flexibility as possible.

Variations include wide-head fluorescent lamps, which deliver an economical and long-lasting illumination, and those designed with a hinged neck and a conventional fabric shade. It has to be said, however, that although these lamps are decorative and capable of giving out an acceptable light by which to read, they are not capable of delivering the finely tuned light of most modern halogen task lamps.

Decorative lighting

Contemporary light designs that perform a purely decorative function have become the latest executive toy, enjoying pride of place in the office or study. Colourful lava lights, whimsical 1960s-style fibre-optic globe lamps and glowing, polypropylene designs are mesmerizing to gaze upon and provide a pleasurable place to rest your eyes between bouts of working on a computer screen.

◄ The latest decorative lamps feature colourful polypropylene designs that emit an eerie glow of light.

bathrooms

Often neglected when it comes to lighting, the bathroom is in fact one of the rooms where good lighting can work wonders. It can transform a mundane "wash-and-go" room into a luxurious sanctuary where you will want to linger and relax. The bathroom is also the perfect place to use chic, high-tech fittings that are decorative focal points in their own right.

The quality of the ambient light must be your first consideration when planning your bathroom lighting scheme. If you have good daylight in your bathroom, make the most of it. No artificial light can quite compare with natural light, which is perfect for applying make-up and shaving by. There are many exciting ways to make the most of daylight – you can install glass bricks, for example, which are architecturally pleasing and allow light to flood into the room while maintaining privacy.

When it comes to artificial lighting, forget the single pendant fitting hanging sadly from the centre of the room and creating gloomy, depressing shadows. Instead, combine several lighting options to flood the bathroom with a warm, luxurious glow, perfect for pampering sessions. Imagine a five-star hotel bathroom and you are on the right lines. Multiple mini low-voltage halogen spots recessed into the ceiling are a good starting point; add a dimmer switch and you can go from clinical brightness to a sensuous warm light, instantly.

Mirrors play a large part in good bathroom design and can be enhanced by clever lighting. A mirror positioned above the basin should therefore be carefully lit. There are many ways to do this, from fitting an integral light source to installing lines of small 25-watt golf-ball lights, set, theatre-style, on either side of the mirror. Used in the right way, mirrors can make a small bathroom feel much roomier. For instance, fix a sheet of mirror to one wall and install wall lights near to it or in front of it. This will produce a clever optical illusion, appearing to double the space and light in the room.

To transform your bathroom from a sparse utilitarian area into a romantic setting, use candles. Set candelabras near the bath, so that their flickering flames are reflected in the water, and add a few scented nightlights to create the ultimate sensual sanctuary.

▼ These white, painted shutters create a high degree of privacy while casting a refreshingly cool light across this bathroom.

▲ To maintain as much light as possible, fit etched glass into the lower panes of glass, or treat with etched glass spray.

Creating more daylight

However good your artificial lighting scheme, there is nothing quite like natural daylight. Natural light is particularly useful in a bathroom, where you need to check your appearance in a "true" light. In addition, walking into the bathroom in the morning to find it bathed in warm sunshine lifts the spirits.

By law, habitable rooms must receive daylight from at least one window, but the bathroom, kitchen and utility areas of the home are exempt from these building regulations. If you do have a window in your bathroom, make the most of it; the perfect place to position the hand basin is beneath a window.

Privacy is obviously an important factor in bathroom design. If your bathroom is overlooked, you will need to create a visual barrier at the window, but this need not block out the sunshine. Fit acid-etched glass to prevent people seeing in while still allowing as much daylight into the room as possible. Alternatively, fasten laminated sheeting or thin white voile over the whole frame. Plain white cotton roller blinds are another contemporary classic that provide privacy yet allow light to enter the room. If your bathroom faces south, you may wish to pull down

the blind whether privacy is a problem or not – the blind will diffuse and cool strong sunshine on a hot summer afternoon, keeping the bathroom pleasantly warm and light but not suffocatingly hot.

Venetian blinds or shutters are another flexible option. The most contemporary style is metallic venetians; some have tiny holes that allow the daylight to filter through and imbue it with a sparkling quality that is very attractive. This looks particularly good in a modern stainless steel and marble bathroom. Left half-open, venetians also create horizontal stripes of light and shade that will lend the bathroom a distinctly Mediterranean mood.

In a period- or traditional-style bathroom, wide wooden slatted blinds or window shutters have a unique appeal. Painted white, they give daylight its fullest expression while providing a colonial setting that suits many decorative styles.

If you have ample space in your bathroom and privacy is not a problem, why not make the most of it by positioning the bath grandly in the centre of the room – with a fancy chandelier overhead? At the window, simple white voile, perhaps decorated with sea shells, will help to create a romantic ambience.

▲ Here, a large window with cotton voile creates a flood of light by day, while at night the room twinkles under the candelabra.

▼ Glass bricks can be used to replace windows; create a shower screen or to "borrow" light from an adjacent room.

It is particularly important that you make the most of the daylight in a compact bathroom or the effect can be gloomy and claustrophobic. It may sound drastic, but if your bathroom adjoins a bedroom, consider knocking down part of the dividing wall and putting up a screen of glass bricks instead. These will allow light to be borrowed from an adjacent bedroom or hallway. Glass bricks now come in a variety of colours. Choose soft ocean blues and greens to simulate the dappled effect of water.

If your bathroom is privately located at the back of the house or has a flat roof, you have two further options. Replace the end window with patio doors so that you can lie in your bath and look out through billowing muslin onto the garden. Alternatively, install a skylight – a particularly inviting prospect if you live in a densely built-up area in the city.

▲ Mirrors make a real difference to the appearance of a small
bathroom and double the effectiveness of the available light.

Colour and texture

Some bathrooms have poor lighting simply because
they do not have sufficient light fittings. A scheme that
uses several lights produces a much better quality of
illumination than a single light source. Use multiple lights
to highlight the different textures and surfaces that are
a key part of the modern bathroom. The stainless steel,
marble and shiny white sanitaryware of loft living all
cry out for the crisp, white light of low-voltage halogen.
However, too much of this intense type of light can cause

▼ A key area for good lighting is above the basin. Here the light has been placed behind the mirror to give excellent illumination.

▲ Tungsten lighting creates a warm glow which is most welcome in a bathroom. This lantern is pierced with star-shaped holes.

▼ Compact fluorescent strips are economical and energy-efficient and burn with a whiter light than traditional tungsten bulbs.

uncomfortable glare – no one wants to lie back in a bath and be blinded by fierce downlighters. To achieve high-intensity light one moment and a comfortable ambient level of illumination the next, fit dimmer switches.

Tungsten is still a favourite choice for period-style bathrooms, where the yellow light creates an atmospheric glow, especially when teamed with warm-coloured wood and the intricate shapes of traditional mouldings and cornicing. Choose pearlized bulbs to achieve a more diffuse effect; clear bulbs cast heavier shadows and make the light source seem smaller.

In a bathroom with a high ceiling, consider a Turkish-style lantern of coloured glass or choose a metal pendant light with holes cut into it that bathe the room in a twinkling light when the lights are dimmed, rather like a mirror ball. Make sure the ceiling is high enough, so that the light is well out of harm's way.

What about fluorescents?

Fluorescents were once the most economical, energy efficient and practical solution for lighting the utilitarian areas of the home, including the bathroom. It was a case of in and out as quickly as possible, which, under the

▼ To illuminate the mirror above the basin with an even flood of shadowless light; place a light source on either side.

brutal greenish glare of a fluorescent tube, was not surprising. But that was then. Over time, bathrooms have developed into key relaxation areas, where we want to pamper ourselves and wallow in aromatherapy oils, surrounded by soft fluffy towels and scented soaps. We need, and expect, good-quality lighting to make bathing a thoroughly enjoyable experience.

In recent years fluorescent lighting has undergone a huge transformation, more so than any other type of lighting. It has been improved and refined markedly. This is partly in response to the need for good-quality energy-saving light sources, a feature for which fluorescents have long been appreciated. The new-generation fluorescents produce a far warmer tone of light than the old ones. They also tend to be smaller and more discreet, so they can be used vertically on walls rather than as one giant strip

overhead. Some have a distinctive 1930s Odeon style, with chrome ends holding a wide tube. A pair of these would make admirable companions either side of a bathroom mirror. Look for fluorescents with a large diffusing filter around the tube so that they cast a soft, low-glare light.

Lighting mirrors

Recessing a light source behind a panel of opaque glass can create anything from a narrow strip to a whole wall of light. Alternatively, a pair of fluorescent tubes concealed by stainless-steel baffles can be installed on either side of a mirror to provide an even illumination across its surface. This quality of light is perfect for shaving, cleaning your teeth and applying make-up.

There are many modern picture lights available in slimline, chrome designs that can be mounted as task

◄ In a tiny washroom use sheets of glass to give the appearance of more space and light with recessed fluorescent strips.

▲ Fluorescent lights can be moulded into circular shapes and used to highlight mirrors or other architectural features.

lights above the bathroom mirror. They have a neat yet glamorous look but do have one significant drawback: lighting a mirror from a single light source positioned above it casts the lower half of the face into heavy shadow, which is far from ideal.

The joy of fluorescent tubes is that they can be shaped and curved to create semicircles or circles of light around a mirror. Not only does this create a good-quality light, it is also a decorative feature in its own right. However, fluorescents cannot be dimmed, so you cannot change the atmosphere of the room with the flick of a switch, as you could with tungsten or halogen lights. If you want to create a softer ambience, you will have to fit a lower wattage fluorescent tube.

If a sense of the theatrical appeals, install rows of golf-ball lights all around the mirror. These generally take the form of several 25- or 40-watt screw-in tungsten bulbs that, when combined, give a high light output. In a contemporary setting with lots of stainless steel or shiny, reflective surfaces, this lighting arrangement can serve to light the whole room.

Perhaps the best light source for a mirror is natural daylight. However, the most common position for a hand

▲ A set of twenty 25W golf ball bulbs outline this large, plate glass mirror and flood the bathroom with light.

basin is below the window, so that the user faces the light – so where does the mirror go? One solution is to install a raised window above the basin. A porthole design would suit a contemporary bathroom and the mirror could then be positioned between the basin and the window. Of course, you will need to include some form of artificial light for using the mirror and basin after dark.

At its simplest, a mirror can be lit with a single tungsten source. A wall light with an extending arm and adjustable head is a neat, practical choice. By using a powerful reflector bulb, you can illuminate a wider area. When shopping for fittings, look for industrial-style, matt, stainless steel designs with concertina extension arms.

◀ Sometimes the simplest ideas are the best. Here a budget, telescopic aluminium task light illuminates a kitsch mirror.

▼ Ask your electrician how many low voltage halogen spotlights you will need. A small bathroom will need around four to six.

▲ Position the downlighters to illuminate the bath, basin and toilet area. Any near the shower should be waterproof.

Concealed sources

In a bathroom, where the ambient light should be soft and glare-free, concealed lighting is a good option. Compact fluorescent strip lighting hidden behind a slim wooden baffle above the basin will enhance the textural quality of nearby materials, such as slate and unpolished marble, without dazzling the eye. Architectural lighting, in the form of low-voltage halogen lights set into the cornicing below the ceiling or recessed into a display cabinet filled with lotions and bath oils, creates a glamorous look.

▼ A narrow alcove which hides all the plumbing is lit by low voltage spots and makes a useful shelf for bottles and cosmetics.

▲ This stunning bathroom has several light sources including glass bricks set into the floor and lit by fluorescent lights from beneath.

Creating a feeling of space

For decades, bathrooms were cheerless places, lit by a single pendant light that was cool and unappealing. It is no wonder they were such depressing rooms – a central pendant casts all the light downwards, throwing out hard shadows but very little ambient light to reach dark corners. Such lighting makes the walls feel as if they are closing in and gives a small bathroom a claustrophobic air.

Effective use of mirrors combined with good lighting can make small bathrooms appear much more roomy. Forget small, individual mirrors; instead, cover whole walls with sheet mirrors. Bear in mind that these will be extremely heavy and require professional installation. Two sheet mirrors placed on opposite walls will give rise to infinite reflections. Install low-voltage downlighters or train spotlights on the mirrors to increase the level of light and feeling of space enormously.

The fundamental design principle for creating the illusion of space involves getting the light to bounce around the walls and off the ceiling. This can be achieved with mirrors or other shiny surfaces. What you are actually doing is using the walls and ceiling as a huge reflector, like a mirror. For this reason you should always paint the ceiling white in a small bathroom, to create better quality light and a feeling of spaciousness. Other shiny surfaces that will help to increase light reflection include marble, granite, ceramic tiles, chrome and glass. Wallwashers, angled spotlights and uplighters, mounted on the walls, are all useful in highlighting these materials. Make sure they are specifically designed for use in bathrooms; that is, generally speaking, with enclosed bulbs.

Under-floor lighting

If you are designing your bathroom from scratch, a novel and exciting lighting scheme is to use floor lights recessed into the ground. One way is to pave the floor with glass bricks, which can then be lit from beneath with hidden fluorescent strips. If your bathroom has a flat roof, this effect can be mirrored with a glass ceiling grid. Although expensive, this arrangement produces a chic-looking bathroom with wonderful ambient light that will be the envy of everyone who comes to visit.

On a more modest level, under-floor lighting can take the form of specially reinforced individual glass spotlights fitted with low-voltage halogen reflectors. Not only do these fittings emit a crisp, white light and good colour

▼ Recessed floor uplighters light up the glass basin. The 6mm
(¼in) thick frosted glass diffusers cover 10W halogen capsules.

▲ If you do not want the hassle of fitting transformers look for
no-fuss, bright 50W mains halogen downlighters with dimmers.

rendering, they also have a lifespan of 3,000 to 3,500
hours. If you are going to the trouble of installing such an
avant-garde arrangement, make the most of it by
positioning the floor lights where they can highlight
interesting features – a glass washstand, for instance.

Use of halogen

The crisp quality of low-voltage halogen light makes it
ideal for bathrooms. Fixed halogen downlighters are
particularly appropriate, since all the main features in
the bathroom are also fixed. The lights can be positioned
to highlight features such as the bath and basin area.
However, fixed downlighters can cause glare, particularly

when lying beneath them in the bath, so it is best to wire
them to a dimmer switch. If your bathroom is large, look
for flood halogen downlighters. These are useful because
they have a beam of light that is 30° or more and therefore
produce a softer wash of light. More versatile, however,
are directable eyeball halogen lights, which can be
adjusted to deflect the light onto the walls, where it will
bounce off and create a softer ambience.

Remember that downlighters do not have to be
installed in the ceiling according to a strict grid pattern.
Use your imagination to create a stylish look – you could
follow the bend of a shower enclosure or the sweep of a
curved wall, for example.

Choosing wall lights

Tungsten light emanating from a pair of wall sconces with
cream shades, placed either side of an ornate mirror, will
create a traditional atmosphere that is both luxurious and
intimate. However, you do not always have to use pairs of
fittings. In a contemporary bathroom, wall lights can be
used as a form of ornament, with each one different and
stylish in its own right. Subtle, curved glass shades that are
set flush with the wall are a space-saving choice for

◀ A smart stainless steel downlighter has been positioned above these glass shelves to create a stunning diplay.

compact bathrooms, while translucent glass and metal uplighters are highly decorative.

If you have enough space in your bathroom, a large shower area can be built into the room using glass bricks. When the shower is lit from within, the bricks will form a large wall of light.

Another stylish option is to fit wall lights into a mirror, so that they appear to float on the sheet of glass. Ask an electrician to mount a large sheet of mirror on the wall, then drill holes in it where you wish to have the lights mounted. Fit them with dimmers so that you can create a relaxing ambience for enjoying a hot soak.

If you prefer architectural-style fittings, wall lights come in a wide variety of designs, from simple plaster curves that can be painted to state-of-the-art polypropylene designs. If you have mosaic walls, you could even cover some plaster wall lights with mosaic tiles, so that they become an integral part of the bathroom design.

◄ Downlighters used to illuminate shower areas need to have a sealed glass cover that is dust and waterproof.

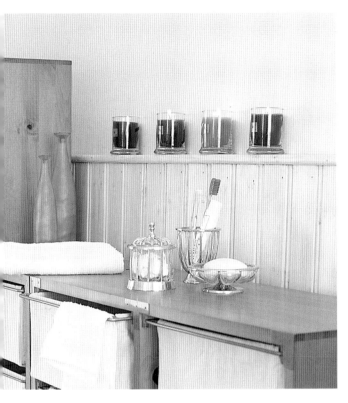

▲ However small your bathroom, find room for a scented candle or two and turn it into a sanctuary.

Using candles

The flickering, golden light of candles can transform a bathroom into a magical place. If you have a wide ledge around the bath, place a couple of candelabras on it, each holding two or three tall candles. The flames will be reflected in the bath water and create a surprising amount of light. If you have mirrored walls around the bath, the reflections from the candles will be multiplied even further, adding to the atmosphere.

Since candles do not require electrical wiring, you can put them wherever you like. Choose from a modern, twisted-metal candelabra mounted on the wall to a bath rack with integral candle holders, so that you can read your magazine in the glow of a flickering flame.

Apart from the area around the sink, bathroom lighting need not be very strong, so candles can be the perfect means to create mood and ambience, especially if you choose scented ones. Even a row of nightlights along the window sill can be enough to set the scene.

Safety in the bathroom

Safety is of paramount importance in any bathroom lighting scheme. Water and electricity are a dangerous combination, so it is vital that you employ a qualified electrician to advise you about fittings and to install the wiring for you. Safety regulations should never be ignored but, since lighting manufacturers offer such a wide range of stylish fittings safe for bathroom use, they will impose only minor limitations on your lighting scheme.

- *Fittings should be positioned at least 2.5m (8ft) away from showers, baths and sinks, unless the metallic parts and bulbs are completely enclosed.*
- *Do not use free-standing floor lamps. These leave cables and wiring on the floor, which, even in a large bathroom, could cause someone to trip and risk putting the light in contact with water.*
- *Adjustable lights are not a good idea in the bathroom, since someone could touch the light fitting with wet hands and suffer an electric shock.*
- *Avoid open pendants or hanging lights with exposed bulbs. These can shatter if splashed with water when hot. They also constitute a potential electrical hazard in such close proximity to water.*
- *Standard socket fittings, switches and lights with flexes should be avoided. Regulations differ depending on which part of the world you are living in. In the United States, where switches are for the most part grounded, normal plate switches can be used inside the bathroom. In the UK, switches are not allowed to be fitted in the bathroom; lights must always be operated by either a pull switch inside the bathroom or a plate switch outside.*

To maximize the level of ambient light, position uplighters high on the walls so that they reflect light off the ceiling. Uplighters are also perfect for highlighting alcoves and recesses. Never use uplighters near the shower area, however, unless they have a waterproof fitting.

Highlighting features

Although the bathroom is primarily a functional room, it should be just as attractive as the other rooms in your home. This means turning your attention to the use of accent lighting to highlight glass shelving, displays of bottles, the area around the bath or even a collection of thick, fluffy towels. A single low-voltage spot set immediately above a set of glass shelves will send an accent light cascading down through the layers of glass, illuminating everything in its path.

If possible, set the bath into an alcove and insert glass shelving backed with sheet mirror at either end. Use accent lighting to highlight coloured perfume bottles and toiletries on the shelves. The simplest method is to install a tungsten strip light, hidden by a wooden panel, but a low-voltage halogen would be even more effective – the narrow, white light source is perfect for making glassware twinkle.

gardens

There is something magical about lighting a garden – done well, it can transform even a modest backyard into a fairytale landscape. Exterior lighting adds a whole new dimension to the home and garden. It is useful for security and for outlining the pathway to your door but is also a powerful decorative tool. Lighting individual plants and features – such as sculptures, ponds and ornaments – will emphasize them and, at the same time, make your garden appear bigger. Outdoor lighting also means you can use your garden after dark in summer.

When lighting a garden, safety is of prime importance and you should ask a qualified electrician to carry out specialized installations for you. All fittings must be weatherproof, to withstand constant exposure to the elements, and, if you are considering lighting a pond, swimming pool or other water feature, the fittings need to be waterproof to withstand immersion.

Cabling, to bring the electrical supply out to the fittings, should be tough and resilient and stringent regulations apply to ensure there is no danger to the public or yourself. Cables are often buried in the soil and this will normally require special conduits. You also need to make sure the cables are protected from lawnmowers and from damage by sharp garden tools.

As for the fittings themselves, these must be kept clear of falling leaves and other garden debris if they are to remain effective. They should be arranged on adjustable switches that can be operated from inside the house.

You can opt for mains-voltage or low-voltage fittings, or a mixture of both. With low-voltage systems, a transformer is required to reduce the voltage from the mains to the required level. The transformer must be protected from the weather and well ventilated. The cabling for mains-voltage systems needs to be buried underground although that for low-voltage fittings does not. Outdoor fittings are labelled to specify their level of resistance to water and dust.

Exterior lighting does not have to be bright to be effective and, in fact, you should guard against "light pollution" – that is, floodlighting in such a way as to dazzle nearby cars or neighbouring homes. The best option for focusing attention on points of interest in the garden is to use subtle, sophisticated illumination.

▼ The colour and quality of the light changes as the sun goes down. Aim to recreate the softness of dusk with tungsten lights.

The quality of light

As the sun slips down the sky at the end of the day, it takes on a deep pink hue and casts long shadows and relaxing, warm pools of light around the garden. Later, when the moon comes out, the light turns a bluer tone, casting cool, silver shades. We are naturally drawn to the warm, rosy colours of sunset – perfect for enjoying an evening glass of wine or a bowl of summer pasta on the patio with friends. It is this quality of light that you should aim to recreate when lighting your garden. Do not be tempted to simulate daylight – the result will be a harsh, overbearing light, not unlike a floodlit baseball pitch.

Light levels should be kept low. Tungsten provides the perfect garden glow while candles and nightlights,

strategically placed, are ideal for lighting a patio or terrace. Keep cooler halogen for accent lighting, perhaps of individual statues and antique, planted urns.

Avoid glaring contrasts between light and shade. Small clusters of light are better than a single strong one – they produce a more balanced effect, particularly if the sources are concealed and positioned at a low level. Just as with interior lighting, garden lighting should be flexible, so install the lights on several different circuits that can be controlled by dimmers.

Lighting an entrance

Although well-lit entrances are a deterrent to burglars, try not to go overboard when lighting the front of your home

▲ Foliage combines with a number of different light sources to create an intriguing, jungle type of feeling to this passageway.

or you will ruin the aesthetics as well as dazzle your guests. In fact, intruders generally break in through concealed side entrances rather than through the front door. Instead of choosing a single overly bright installation, opt for several less-intense light sources to create a stylish and welcoming entrance. The effect will be much improved if you can blend the lights into the foliage while still illuminating the approach to your home.

If you have a narrow approach, create an intriguing setting by covering the walls with trellis and trailing creepers over it. You can then intersperse outdoor uplighter and downlighter fittings among the plants, both at ground level and along the walls. They will highlight the foliage with a pleasant, dappled effect. This lighting scheme works best if you paint the walls white, which creates a pleasing contrast with the glossy green leaves.

◀ Spotlights can be recessed into the path itself to highlight both the route and specimen plants.

illumination. This has the effect of casting soft washes of light up the walls of the building.

The softer and more numerous the light sources, the more romantic the effect will be. The lighting should subtly highlight the texture of mouldings, columns, shutters, ornate barge boards and other artistic details. Good lighting will reveal fascinating nooks and crannies, create intriguing shadows and can even make the building look larger and grander. Conversely, bad lighting will flatten out any contrasts and neutralize the beauty of the architecture in one bland sweep of light. In many ways, bad floodlighting is worse than no lighting at all.

Avoid directing the exterior lighting into the rooms of your home at all costs. This will create a visual eyesore from the outside and a badly lit interior on the inside, rather like living too close to a city street light.

Lighting pathways

A clever lighting scheme can divide your garden into a number of areas, which can then be linked by pathways twinkling with light. A common mistake, however, is to use overpowering, insensitive lighting – the idea is to enhance, not dazzle. Lit properly, illuminated walkways are a delightful decorative tool for enhancing the colour, texture and depth of nearby plants and shrubbery as well as of the paving material itself.

One of the simplest methods is to insert outdoor uplighters with integral spikes into the grass that flanks the path. Make sure any cabling is carried in weatherproof conduits and buried deep in the ground where it cannot be damaged by lawnmowers or digging. If there is little foliage on either side of the path, choose small lights – they will still create a good illumination.

Alternatively, recess spotlights into the path itself. If protected by a safety glass shield, they can be covered with gravel to produce glowing, diffuse circles of light. They look particularly attractive when following the outline of a meandering path.

On a more dramatic scale, you can create an ornamental promenade of climbing plants, growing up a series of metal arches. Wind twinkling fairy lights around the arches to create a magical effect; an illuminated statue at the end of the walkway will add the finishing touch. Look for waterproof lights that are specially designed for outside use and have them fitted by a qualified electrician who specializes in garden lighting – never be tempted to use indoor fairy lights.

If you have an attractive period portico, an overhead coach lamp will enhance the setting. These lights can look out of place on modern or contemporary homes, however, where the best choice is a simple globe light or practical bulk-head fitting.

Art deco or 1960s-style houses often feature sheet glass as part of the front porch. These can be illuminated from within – with a series of mini-fluorescent strips, for example – to create a most effective entrance light. This device works best if the glass is sandblasted or etched – it creates a radiant panel of diffuse light that will enhance the austere architectural lines of the porch.

Floodlighting buildings

If your home has decorative architectural features, such as porticos, columns or a textured facade, floodlighting – when properly executed, of course – can transform it into a fairytale vision. There is definitely a secret to getting it right, however; if overdone, the effect can resemble the worst kind of supermarket floodlighting. As with so many things, less is more. The best examples of highlighted architecture are those where the light sources are hidden among dense banks of foliage to soften and diffuse the

▲ This ornamental avenue was created by training small trees over metal arches and winding outdoor fairylights around them.

When lighting steps, a series of low-level lights set into the raisers or an adjacent wall will highlight both the pathway and the textural quality of the stone or paving. For a quick transformation, place nightlights in terracotta jars on each step, perfect for a summer party to light the way to a dance area or terrace.

Lighting patios and terraces

Terraces and patios require a higher level of illumination than the other parts of the garden, particularly if you are planning to eat there. Being near to the house, however, you can "borrow" light from interior rooms. If you have an awning or some type of roofing over the eating area, you

▲ A meadow of knee-deep grass becomes a dining room lit by table candles and lanterns hanging from overhead trees.

can hang additional overhead lighting from it as well as keep out the rain. You have the choice of spotlights or simple pendants. For the latter, choose pretty Chinese-style lanterns that will sway gently in the evening breeze. Use low-wattage bulbs and supplement the lighting with candles and flares to create more atmosphere.

On the table, candles are the most evocative lighting choice. If you use enough, you can create sufficient illumination to dine by candlelight alone, which means you can position the table anywhere, not just on the terrace – imagine a romantic candlelit table in a meadow of tall, sweet-smelling wild flowers. To increase the level of ambient light, hang overhead lanterns securely from an adjacent tree and highlight each place setting with nightlights in delicate glass holders. Complete the scene with a centrepiece of floating candles and flowerheads in a large bowl; citronella-scented candles are the best choice because they also act as an insect repellent. Of course,

◄ Citronella-scented torches will not only give out a good light when "planted" around the garden, but also ward off bugs.

▲ Trees can look quite unearthly when lit from beneath with mains voltage tungsten in the form of spiked garden uplights.

for the ultimate in the theatrical, the choice has to be flares, which are now widely available.

Lighting plants

There is something indefinably pleasing about the combination of lighting and green leaves – the light enhances the texture of the plants and shines through the foliage to highlight the different shades of green. Even the humblest plant takes on a statuesque elegance when lit from beneath by a concealed light source. Similarly, trees can look ghostly and ethereal when lit with ground spotlights angled upwards.

The most common form of garden lighting are spiked lamps that use mains-voltage tungsten via underground cabling. They can be angled to shine exactly where you need them, highlighting your favourite plants and trees as required. Most use fairly large "flood" bulbs, so they need to be concealed among plants to avoid creating a brutal glare, which will destroy any mystical atmosphere you are trying to produce. You can also fit them with coloured lenses to achieve different effects. Blue will enhance the look of moonlight while green will reinforce the appearance of healthy foliage. Two or three lamps set in a dense border of foliage will create a delightful effect, even

▼ Bamboo poles hung with lanterns provide effective romantic lighting in your garden without the trouble of laying cables.

▲ Winter, when the trees are bare, is the perfect time to drape the branches with waterproof, weather-resistant coloured bulbs.

▲ You can light your patio from the inside out. This glass roof means further outside lighting is superfluous.

in a small garden. They are ideal for lighting trees and large shrubs and can simply be inserted into the ground wherever you want them, once the cabling has been laid.

There are various ways to light large trees. Lit from the front, the upper part of a tall tree may be thrown into darkness but the trunk and lower area of foliage will be highlighted. This is particularly suitable if you wish to highlight a feature suspended from the tree, such as a hanging lantern or decorative birdhouse. Backlighting a tree – by placing the light source behind it – will give rise to a dramatic silhouette and is probably the best way to emphasize the tree's shape and texture.

It is possible to bathe a garden in enchanting light quickly and with very little expenditure. Buy half a dozen bamboo poles and hang a small metal lantern from each one, containing a nightlight or candle. Insert the poles into the ground in a group, ideally surrounded by lush vegetation, to transform the garden into an eastern island paradise. It creates the perfect party setting, but why not just enjoy it for yourself?

In winter, when deciduous trees lose their leaves, lighting can have different effects again. Uplighting makes bare tree branches gleam with light after a fall of rain.

Alternatively, use colour to create imaginative effects – trail small orange and red bulbs through the branches or hang miniature low-voltage lights from them in various shades of blue. Make sure the lights are waterproof and the weather-resistant cabling is fully submerged.

Roof gardens

Roof gardens, by virtue of their dizzy heights, have a magic all of their own. Add good lighting and you have a unique, fantasy setting. Obviously, cabling cannot be concealed easily without flowerbeds, which are usually far too heavy for a roof to support. However, you can get a professional electrician to lay the cabling in discreet conduits along the side of the building; position uplighters or low-level diffused lights at strategic intervals to highlight a few exotic plants in large, attractive pots. If a glass roof or window is adjacent to the roof garden, the borrowed light could be sufficient to light the whole area, which is usually fairly small.

Keep to a green and white theme to create a sophisticated design that works well with the bright, interior halogen lights of a modern home. White walls surrounding the roof terrace will make the most of the

▲ Statues, urns and walled features look stunning at night when lit. Position the lights to maximize the texture and form.

▶ This simple waterspout and pebble feature looks stunning when lit. However, special waterproof fittings need to be used.

available light by bouncing it around in all directions; complete the effect with white flowering shrubs.

Lighting statues and features

Architectural and decorative features with interesting shapes and textures are ideal subjects for garden accent lighting. An ancient urn with trailing ivy, a statue of a Greek goddess, a stone bird bath or a garden seat – all are worthy of the added emphasis that accent lighting will give. In nearly all cases, the feature looks best when lit from beneath. This throws light up against the object, highlighting its texture and shape and giving it a golden outline against the night sky. Larger features, such as an archway in a wall, may need two or more lights for effective illumination.

Both tungsten and halogen can be used to highlight garden features. Tungsten will enhance the colour of brickwork with a beautiful golden hue but halogen also has its place – miniature low-voltage fixtures hidden among a collection of small flowerpots around a larger, central planter throw up discreet shafts of white light that will highlight the display attractively.

▼ Ten waterproof, tungsten spotlights, permanently submerged in the water, are used to light this elegant statue and waterfall.

Lighting water features

Water features deserve special attention when it comes to garden lighting. Probably the most evocative way is to light the water from beneath the surface, using specially designed waterproof fittings. If you combine the effect of moving water with light, the result is even more miraculous, so never pass up the chance to illuminate a waterfall or fountain. It does not matter whether your water feature is large or small. At one end of the scale, a large floodlit pool surrounded by species trees, uplit from beneath, has a truly glamorous effect. The blueness of the pool will be greatly enhanced by adding blue filters to the underwater light fittings. However, equally beguiling is a small wall fountain lit by a pair of spotlights – it is the simplicity that is so appealing.

Safety in the garden

Garden light fittings must be durable and able to withstand changing weather conditions, including rain and extremes of temperature. It is therefore vital that all safety regulations affecting garden lighting are strictly adhered to.

- *Light fittings must be waterproof and corrosion-proof. Check that any exterior lights you buy are marked with a special IP (ingress protection) code, which consists of two numbers. The first number indicates how well insulated the light is against airborne contamination – dust, for example – on a scale of 0 to 6. The second number indicates how waterproof the fitting is, ranging from 0 for zero protection through drip-, splash-, rain- and jet-proof up to a maximum rating of 8, which indicates that the light can be immersed in water at pressure.*
- *Cabling carrying mains-voltage electricity to outdoor light installations must be specially armoured.*
- *Mains-voltage cabling should be buried at least 45cm (18in) underground, deeper if it passes under areas of the garden where digging takes place.*
- *Low-voltage cabling does not have to be buried.*
- *Both mains- and low-voltage cabling must be heatproof and waterproof.*
- *For suspended lighting, overhead cables must be at least 3.5m (11ft) off the ground and supported at intervals of 3.5m (11ft).*
- *Outdoor sockets must be weatherproof and covered.*
- *All outdoor lighting installations should be carried out by a professional electrician.*

practicalities

Before you choose your light fittings, you need to decide what type of light source – or bulb – you want. The three main forms are tungsten, fluorescent and halogen. Each has its own characteristics, including the colour of light it emits, colour rendering properties, longevity and cost.

Light is a form of electromagnetic radiation. Although we see natural light as white, it is in fact made up from a spectrum of colours, each with a different wavelength. If you shine light through a prism, you will see it break up into its component wavelengths, each with a different colour, like a rainbow.

Depending at what temperature a filament, gas or wick is glowing, it will emit a different coloured light. The higher the temperature (measured in degrees Kelvin), the whiter (or "cooler") the light. This varies from a candle – which burns at just 2000° Kelvin and gives out a warm, golden glow – to direct sunlight – which burns at around 5500° Kelvin at midday and is the whitest light of all. Artificial lighting includes a wide spectrum of temperatures between these two extremes, giving rise to the characteristics associated with each type of light bulb.

The higher the temperature, the whiter or cooler the light and the better that colours can be seen when illuminated by it – this attribute is known as colour rendering. This is why colours look their truest shade when seen in daylight.

In the golden glow of candlelight – and to a lesser extent tungsten lighting – colours are distorted by a bias towards the red/orange part of the spectrum. Fluorescent lighting also has its drawbacks. Although it burns at a higher temperature than tungsten and emits a white light, it has peaks in the green/yellow part of the spectrum, which is why it can give skin tones a sickly pallor. Halogen lighting, burning at the highest temperature bar sunlight, gives coloured objects their truest interpretation. Originally designed for commercial settings such as restaurants and shops, halogen is now increasingly being enjoyed in domestic lighting installations.

Once you have decided on the type of bulb, it is time to shop for fittings. These are multifarious but divide into several basic categories, which we will examine in turn. They include table lamps, floor lamps, downlighters, uplighters, wall lights, task lights, pendant lights, tracks and, finally, a newcomer – bare-wire installations.

▼ A crown-silvered tungsten bulb gives out a less direct beam than an ordinary bulb.

▲ A tiny low voltage 50W dichroic lamp using 12volts produces an intense bright light.

▲ Large PAR38 tungsten spotlights have been superceded by low voltage halogen.

▼ Compact fluorescents are an economical choice and the latest developments have been improved to give out a less sickly tone.

Bulbs

Most artificial light is produced by either incandescence or fluorescence. Incandescence occurs when an electric current passes through a metal filament, causing it to heat up and glow. Incandescent bulbs include tungsten, tungsten-halogen (also known simply as halogen) and low-voltage halogen.

Fluorescence occurs when electricity is passed through a gas-filled tube or bulb and the gas particles vibrate, producing an invisible radiation that then reacts with a phosphor coating within the tube, causing it to glow. This takes place at low temperatures, so less energy is consumed. Since there is no filament to burn out, fluorescent bulbs never blacken or suddenly fail but they will fade gradually over time.

Examining the main attributes of the three main types of bulb will help you to decide which type of lighting, and indeed fitting, is most appropriate for your requirements.

Tungsten bulbs: A standard 100-watt tungsten bulb burns at 2700° Kelvin. The colour of the light is whiter than that of a candle but still has distinctly warm, yellowish overtones that are relaxing and easy on the eye. Tungsten has the shortest lifespan of all light sources – a mere 1,000 hours – and, although tungsten bulbs are the most commonly available and are cheap to buy, this form of lighting is actually expensive to run. As well as being available in the classic bulb shape, tungsten can also be produced in tube or strip form. So-called long-lasting tungsten bulbs are available with stronger filaments and special internal gases to prevent blackening. However, they are expensive and the light output is lower. Tungsten lighting can be dimmed.

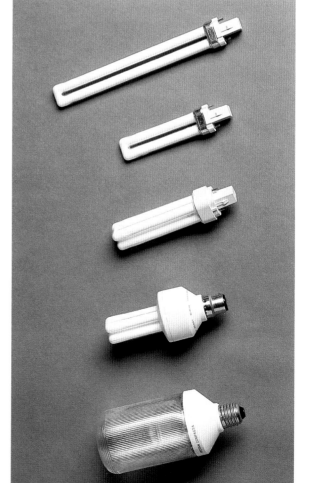

▼ Small, pearl or clear, round tungsten bulbs are available with either bayonet or screw fittings in 25, 40 and 60 watts.

▲ Fluorescent tubes are still used in bathroom and kitchen settings, to light mirrors and worksurfaces

Fluorescent bulbs: Fluorescent lights can burn at anything from 2500–5000° Kelvin; the original 1930s versions burned at the higher end of this scale and produced a white light. However, the trouble with fluorescent lighting is its characteristic peaks in the green/yellow area of the spectrum, so although the light is "cool", its attendant colour distortions give a sickly hue to skin tones and interior decoration. Contemporary fluorescents burn at a lower temperature, which produces a warmer, more flattering tone of light, particularly when concealed behind wood or opal glass baffling. Fluorescent bulbs have a very long lifespan of 8,000 hours and are economical and energy efficient. These low operating costs make them popular for commercial settings. Fluorescent lighting cannot be dimmed.

Tungsten-halogen bulbs: Finally, tungsten-halogen (also generally known as halogen) lights – a relatively new development – burn at around 3000° Kelvin, which gives the light a far crisper, bright white (or cooler) colour and good colour rendering. As the name suggests, halogen is the extra ingredient. Mixed with the other gases within the bulb, halogen reacts with the evaporated tungsten to prolong the life of the bulb and prevent blackening, while allowing the filament to burn at a higher temperature. Halogen bulbs are far smaller than tungsten ones, with wattages up to around 700 watts. There are two types:

Mains-voltage halogen bulbs have a lifespan of up to 5,000 hours. They provide the light quality and brilliance of a quartz capsule, but operate at mains voltage. Like tungsten, however, they have poor energy efficiency because they generate a lot of heat and are therefore more expensive to buy and to run. They can be dimmed.

Low-voltage halogen lighting has given rise to a revolution in modern interior domestic lighting, having first appeared in retail outlets. The bulbs have the same general characteristics as the mains-voltage version, but are made of quartz, rather than glass, to withstand the higher temperatures. The advantage is that they are much smaller, giving a discreet light source capable of delivering a highly focused beam. They are also more energy efficient and cheaper to operate because the wattages are lower – from 15 to 50 watts. The disadvantage is that they need a transformer, but they are dimmable. Because of the low voltage, they can safely be suspended from unprotected wires on so-called bare-wire installations, creating stylish and high-tech effects for modern interiors.

▲ Even traditional tungsten lamps now look chic and modern. The base of this design is a work of art in itself.

▲ More contemporary lamp designs are breaking away from the traditional base-and-shade idea and feature "tubes" of light.

Table lamps

Table lamps are perhaps the most common light fitting apart from the pendant, and as such, are often passed over with merely a cursory glance. However, they have more to offer than you might at first think. Table lamps are excellent light sources and come in many shapes, styles and sizes, and can be fitted with an enormous range of lamp shades. Each of these elements of a table lamp's design has a dramatic influence on its effectiveness in different situations.

The classic table lamp includes a base with a shade suspended over the light source, originating from a candlestick design. When selecting this arrangement, it is essential to get the proportions right; the wider the bottom of the shade, the broader the area of illumination and the wider the base can be. To light the area beneath the lamp most effectively, combine a narrow base with a wide shade.

If the shade is transparent, it will also give out horizontal light, which is vital if you intend to use a series of lamps to create the ambient light in a room. Choose a white or pale shade to achieve a warm light without casting the room with an unnatural tint. An opaque or

black shade is perfect when you want to illuminate only the area beneath the lamp; such shades are the obvious choice for bedside tables.

Traditional table lamp designs have more recently given way to high-tech and contemporary styles that resemble works of art. Lamp designers are now creating bases from textural materials such as frosted glass, paper and moulded plastics and combining them with beaded, over-wrapped silk, velvet and fake fur shades.

Floor lamps

Until fairly recently, "standard" or floor lamps had a rather old-fashioned and out-moded image. A new generation of floor lamps, however, is paving the way for ever more stylish and contemporary designs. Some of them are almost sculptural in their appeal – some stunning examples are available in the form of tall columns of paper or plastic lit from within by multiple bulbs, creating an elegant monolith of light. Best news of all, the new designs are increasingly available at affordable prices. These stylish lights are the perfect solution for loft-style open living spaces, since they are imposing enough not to be dwarfed by the dimensions of a large warehouse apartment.

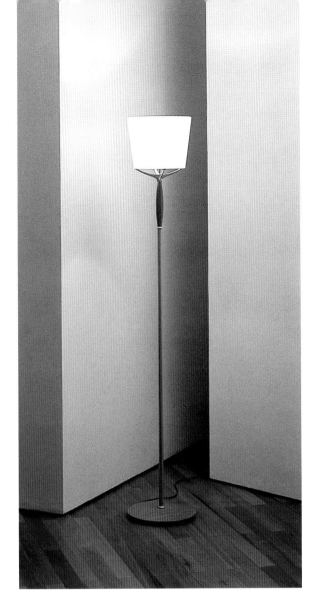

▲ A minimalist floor-standing lamp throws the light up and away creating an attractive, diffuse ambient light.

Downlighters

Downlighters cast their illumination in a downward path from high above. They do not include pendant lights, however, which are defined as a separate category. Downlighters are discreet, fitted lights recessed into a horizontal surface, such as the ceiling, but they can also include lights mounted locally into shelving or a wall unit above a kitchen work surface. They can be totally or partially recessed. Fully recessed, they require a minimum of 12.5cm (5in) of ceiling space to accommodate the fitting and ensure adequate ventilation. If this is not possible, surface-mounted fittings are available.

You can choose from mains-voltage tungsten for a warm yellow light; fluorescent strips concealed in a ceiling recess; mains-voltage halogen for a cooler effect and better colour rendering; or the twinkling, miniature fixtures of low-voltage halogen capsules fitted with dichroic reflectors, which reflect the light forward while transmitting heat through the back of the fitting. Downlighters should always be installed by a qualified electrician, to ensure that they are adequately ventilated and to avoid a fire hazard.

Downlighters can be static – that is, fixed in position – or directional. The former is a reasonable choice for bathrooms and kitchens, where the sanitaryware, units and most of the furniture is itself fixed. However, in a living room, where you may wish to change your seating arrangement or adjust the position of your furniture to suit

Of course, there are more classic designs available, too. Some have their roots in the traditional brass or wooden standard lamp with its pleated silk shade. However, their image has also been updated, leaving behind the fussy frills and tassels of their forerunners.

Some examples feature the latest in 21st-century materials, namely acid-etched glass, polypropylene, brightly coloured plastics, stainless steel and textured papers, which have a translucence that is perfect for emitting a soft, diffuse light.

Some modern floor lamps also retain the flexibility of the traditional designs, but now with snake-head, bendable necks, extending vertical metal columns and even telescopic arms to focus over the back of a chair or extend over a table. While floor lamps are usually fitted with tungsten bulbs to emit a warm, relaxing glow, some of the neater, more contemporary designs feature compact halogen bulbs that deliver an accurate beam of bright white light, which is the perfect choice for reading by.

▼ This downlighter features a two-tiered glass design which helps to diffuse the light and looks stunning.

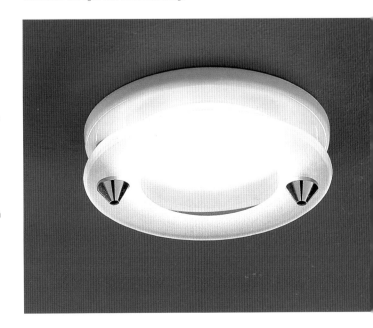

◄ This contemporary uplighter features a sweeping dish of opaque glass which throws the light up to create a diffuse effect.

the seasons, flexible downlighters such as eyeball spots are a good idea, particularly if fitted with dimmer switches.

Uplighters

Uplighters work in the opposite way to downlighters: they throw light up towards the ceiling, where it is reflected back down into the room in the form of a gentle, unfocused light with few harsh shadows. Because of this diffuse quality, uplighters are an indispensable way of creating good-quality ambient lighting in a variety of interiors. They are perfect for use in studies and workrooms where intense visual concentration is required.

High ceilings work well with uplighters because the light has a chance to spread out before being reflected off the ceiling, which produces a gentler, more dilute effect. Architectural details can also benefit from this type of lighting – the uplighters will highlight any coving, cornicing or mouldings to their best advantage. Textured walls including bricks, raw plaster and stucco can be beautifully emphasized by a series of uplighters around the edge of a room. Conversely, of course, damaged or inferior quality plaster will not pass the scrutiny of uplighters.

Uplighters can also be used as accent lights, to draw attention to a picture, large sculpture or collection of artefacts. If the uplighter is small and placed on the floor, it can be hidden behind a desk or chair with just the beam of light visible, radiating up to illuminate the object, throwing it into relief and emphasizing its texture and form. The joy of floor-standing uplighters is that they can be unplugged and moved easily, which makes them extremely flexible. Wall-mounted uplighters, by contrast, are fixed permanently in position, so consider the alternatives before you have them installed.

Spotlights

The first spotlights entered the domestic arena back in the 1960s. They contain a reflector bulb that directs a beam of light with an angle of less than 30°. By contrast, a "flood" reflector bulb is one that emits a beam of light that is greater than 30°.

Spotlights have their origins in the theatre, so it comes as no surprise that even the most minimalist spotlight will add a sense of drama to an interior. A spotlight's job is to highlight features and areas with an uncompromising shaft of light that creates dazzling illumination.

Spotlights can be wall-mounted, fitted to the ceiling, angled from a vertical metal pole, clipped onto a nearby

▼ More and more low voltage halogen spots are being set into floors. You find them illuminating stairs, hallways and bathrooms.

▼ Low voltage downlighters are all compact and neat. Choose from glass, gold or stainless steel; fixed or eyeball sockets.

▲ This trio of low voltage halogen downlighters are mounted on moveable snakes' head arms for ultimate flexibility.

▲ The humble pendant fitting takes on a whole new look with these stunning aluminium designs used as a pair.

vertical surface or secured to a bedhead. The variations are infinite. If you wish to create an intense, pinpoint beam of pure white light – for illuminating a miniature, small sculpture or a discreet work area, for instance – use a spotlight fitted with a low-voltage halogen bulb.

For a wider spread of light – for highlighting a bookcase or for use at the bedside, for example – the best choice is a tungsten spotlight fitted with a reflector bulb. The bulbs are silvered on the inside to help throw the beam of light forward. Bear in mind, however, that mini-tungsten spotlights often do not take bulbs above 40 watts, which can give a disappointingly insipid light output over any distance.

The strength of the bulb is not the only factor to affect the level of illumination. The style of the fitting also has a strong influence: some spotlights have shutters, others have filters, diffusers or even "barn doors" – a theatre lighting term for the adjustable flaps that are used to direct the beam of a spotlight.

Pendant lights

For many designers, pendant lights – overhead hanging lights – are the most dismal choice in artificial lighting. At first glance, it is easy to see why – a single, hanging light casts a bright beam of light directly beneath it while leaving the far corners of the room in gloom. Anyone standing beneath the pendant would have part of his or her face cast into deep shade, their cheeks and eye sockets hollowed with shadows. The way the light falls from a pendant means that any architectural features above the light source are invisible; to look up is to risk being dazzled by the light source itself. In addition, decorative features that fall within the spread of light are washed with a bland, characterless illumination that negates any possibility of an intimate atmosphere.

However, there *is* a redeeming side to the much-maligned pendant fitting, as long as it is used correctly. Probably the most useful place to hang a pendant is above a dining table. Hung low, the pendant will illuminate the

▲ Most modern low voltage task light designs have an integral transformer fitted into the base of the lamp itself,

▲ This state-of-the-art task light directs a narrow beam of white light and is finely adjustable by virtue of the counter-balance.

surface immediately beneath it, while the faces of the diners remain beyond the flood of light. One of the most attractive arrangements is to hang a series of two or more compact pendants over the table, especially if they are fitted with coloured glass shades and lit with bright halogen bulbs.

In a bathroom, where a fully enclosed bulb is necessary, a pendant can also have a place – a glass globe will create a good ambient light, for example. In fact, nearly all pendants benefit from concealing the light source. This can be achieved either by fitting the light with an enclosed shade or by choosing a pendant where the bulb is well recessed. Crown-silvered bulbs, which reflect the light upwards, are also a good way to reduce glare immediately beneath the light.

Task lights

The most common form of task lights are reading lights and desk lights. Task lights are designed to throw a highly focused beam of light onto a nearby work surface, the page of a book or a computer keypad. Designs of task lights have developed rapidly in recent years, due to the advent of compact, low-voltage halogen bulbs. However,

there is still a place for the classical greats – you can still purchase the Anglepoise in its original 1934 form or a 1950s-style Bestlite.

Contemporary designs are also highly successful at combining form and function. The latest task lights feature cantilevered arms to balance the light source in exactly the right position; bendable metal arms that are infinitely adjustable; jointed and tensioned extensions; or no-nonsense telescopic limbs. These devices are all aimed at making the lights flexible, and are adept at delivering the right light exactly where it is needed.

You can select the yellow glow of tungsten for your bedside reading lamp or a relaxed study, but most of the new-age task lights are lit with low-voltage halogen. The benefits are two-fold: the size of the bulb is so compact that the lamp itself can be of neat, minimalist design, plus the bulb produces a concentrated, bright white light that is the perfect quality for concentrated work without the problems of glare.

▼ There's no denying the appeal of low voltage halogen. A high-tech solution, they look sleek and give out an excellent light.

▲ Track fittings are a good choice for kitchens where the low voltage spots can be angled exactly where they are needed.

▲ This track lighting shows two examples of low voltage halogen spots. The one of the left has "barn doors" to reduce glare.

Track lights and bare-wire installations

Track lighting originated in the late 1960s and over the last 20 years or so has undergone some startling updates that have become popular in the lighting designs of domestic interiors. There are two basic formats. The first is the "fixed" form, in which the track is sold as a package with two, three or four mains-voltage light fittings fixed in position. These lights can be angled and directed in different orientations, but they cannot be moved along the length of the track. Such lights are readily available and relatively inexpensive.

In its latest incarnation, however, track has gone "free-form". The electrical supply travels to the track or "bus bar" through protected conduits so that the track itself becomes an extended power source. Lights can be plugged into or unplugged from the track as required. With such an arrangement, the same track can be used to power a pendant in one part of the room and a series of downlighters in another. Free-form tracks can be powered by both high and low voltage. High-voltage tracks usually

have a transformer hidden in the ceiling space, while low-voltage tracks generally include an integral transformer. Tracking can go anywhere – in linear arrangements up walls and across ceilings or in elegant (but expensive) curves that snake across the ceiling. The main disadvantage of track lighting is the risk of overloading the system; low-voltage installations are particularly vulnerable. Always make sure you do not add more lights than the rating on the transformer dictates.

Very much a recent development, so-called "bare-wire" installations go one step further than track lighting, in conjunction with the development of low-voltage halogen. Because the lights are powered by only 12 volts, unsheathed electrical wires can safely be touched and suspended at high tension between the walls, or between the floor and the ceiling. From these wires the miniature low-voltage capsules or dichroic reflectors are suspended and can be moved freely to exactly where they are required. This produces a contemporary lighting installation that is simple and the perfect solution for the large, open living spaces of converted warehouses and loft apartments.

directory of suppliers

Aero
96 Westbourne Grove
London W2 5RT

Modern wall and floor lamps.

After Noah
121 Upper Street
London N1 1QP

Quirky second-hand lighting.

Aktiva
8 Berkley Road
London NW1 8YR

Low voltage halogen lighting.

Angelic
194 Kings Road
London SW3 5ED

Candles and candlesticks.

Ann's of Kensington
34a/b Kensington Church
Street, London W8 4HA

*Lampshades and bases.
Shades made to order.*

Aram Designs
3 Kean Street
London WC2B 4AT

*Modern designer lighting
including Flos and Arteluce.*

Ruth Aram Shop
65 Heath Street
London NW3 6UG

Fun trendy modern lighting.

Artemide GB Ltd
323 City Road
London EC1V 1LJ

*Italian lighting. Trade supplier
call for retail outlets.*

Atrium
Centrepoint
22–24 St Giles High Street
London WC2H 8LN

*Importers of top European
lighting and mail order.*

Beaumont & Fletcher Ltd
261 Fulham Road
London SW3 6HY

*Regency- and Georgian-style
lighting.*

Babylon Designs
Unit 7 New Inn Square
1 New Inn Street
London EC2A 3PY

*Modern designs and designers.
Trade supplier call for retailers.*

Basis Design Ltd
Unit 17–18, 109 Bartholomew
Road, London NW5 2BJ

*Good modern lighting. Trade
supplier call for retail outlets.*

Bella Figura
Decoy Farm Old Church Road
Melton
Suffolk IP13 6DH and

G5 Chelsea Harbour Design
Centre
London SW10 0XE

*Traditional decorative lighting
and lampshades to order.*

Besselink Jones & Milne
99 Walton Street
London SW3 2HH

*Table lamps, picture light
pendants and storm lanterns.*

Best & Lloyd
William Street
West Smethwick
Warley
West Midlands B66 2NX

*Manufacturers of the famous
'Bestlite'. Picture lights, swing-
arm lamps and chandeliers
made to measure. Trade
supplier call for retailers.*

Box Products
Unit 296 Oxo Tower
Wharf Barge House Street
London SE1 9PH

*Custom-made lighting plus
metal and glass designs.*

BHS Plc
129-137 Marylebone Road
London NW1 5QD

*Traditional and contemporary
lighting at affordable prices.*

Candela Ltd
51 Abbey Business Centre
Ingate Place
London SW8 3NS

*Classic minimalist low voltage
halogen lighting.*

**Capital Electrical
Wholesalers**
38 Goldhawk Road
London W12 8DH

*Good selection of light
fittings. Trade supplier call for
retail outlets.*

Catalytico
25 Montpelier Street
London SW7 1HF

*Lighting by Ingo Maurer and
Luceplan among others. Trade
supplier call for retail outlets.*

Chelsea Lighting Design
Unit 1 23a Smith Street
London SW3 4EJ

*Custom-made designer
lighting from across Europe.
Traditional and modern styles.*

Christopher Hyde
Unit 4 Vulcan Business Centre
18 Vulcan Way
Croydon
Surrey CR0 9UG

*Outdoor lanterns; ceramic and
terracotta table lamps. Trade
supplier call for retail outlets.*

Christopher Wray
199 Shaftesbury Avenue
London WC2H 8JR

*The largest traditional lighting
UK showroom. Contemporary
styles also available.*

The Conran Shop
Michelin House
81 Fulham Road
London SW3 6RD

Modern lighting designs.

Designer Light Shop
4 Kennington Road
London SE1 7BL

*Wide range of contemporary
designers including Flos
Arteluce and Foscarini.*

Erco Lighting Ltd
38 Dover Street
London W1X 3RB

*Contemporary architectural-
style lighting. Trade supplier
call for retail outlets.*

**Electrical Contractors
Association**
34 Palace Court
London W2 4HY

*Contact for a list of approved
electrical contractors.*

Elizabeth Eaton
86 Bourne Street
London SW1W 8UP

Traditional lighting.

The Facade
196 Westbourne Grove
London W11 2RH

*Antique lighting including
French chandeliers, table lights
and frosted glass shades.*

**Fergus Cochrane & Leigh
Warren**
570 Kings Road
London SW6 2DY

*French crystal chandeliers from
1800 onwards.*

Flos
31 Lisson Grove
London NW1 6UV

*Agents for Arteluce Philippe
Starck and Castiglioni. Trade
supplier call for retail outlets.*

Forbes and Lomax
205b St John's Hill
London SW11 1TH

*Manufacturers of the 'invisible'
perspex switch plus brass and
stainless steel switches, toggles
and dimmers.*

Fritz Fryer Antique Lighting
12 Brookend Street
Ross-on-Wye
Herefordshire HR9 7EG

*Traditional styles from 1800 to
1920. Design and restoration.*

Fulham Kitchens
18 Carnwath Road
London SW6 3HR

Specialists in kitchen lighting.

**Garden Lighting
Installations**
Argent Court Hook Rise South
Tolworth, Surrey KT6 7LD

*Outdoor lighting systems
including underwater lights.*

Habitat
196 Tottenham Court Road
London W1P 9LD

*Good range of affordable
contemporary lighting.*

Hamilton Litestat Group
Quarry Industrial Estate
Mere, Wiltshire BA12 6LA

*Trade supplier of light switch
plates, call for retail outlets.*

Heal's
196 Tottenham Court Road
London W1P 9LD

Modern lighting styles.

Hector Finch Lighting
88 Wandsworth Bridge Road
London SW6 2TF

Antique lighting specialists.

Hemisphere
173 Fulham Road
London SW3 6JW

*Retro-style 1940s and 1950s
lighting designs.*

Guzzini Illuminazione UK Ltd
Unit 3 Mitcham Industrial Estate
85 Streatham Road
Mitcham, Surrey CR4 2AP

*Modern lighting. Trade supplier
call for retail outlets.*

IKEA (Head Office)
2 Drury Way
North Circular Road
London NW10 0TH

*Affordable contemporary and
traditional lighting.*

Inflate
3rd Floor, 5 Old Street
London EC1V 9HL

Funky inflatable lighting. Trade supplier call for retail outlets.

In House
28 Howe Street
Edinburgh EH3 6TG
Tel: 0131 225 2888 and
24–26 Wilson Street
Glasgow G1 1SS

Contemporary lighting styles.

John Cullen Lighting
585 Kings Road
London SW6 2EH

Contemporary lighting plus made-to-measure systems.

John Lewis Partnership
Oxford Street
London W1A 1EX

Traditional and contemporary light fittings and accessories.

Kensington Lighting Co
59 Kensington Church Street
London W8 4HA

Crystal and metal chandeliers.

Liberty
214 Regent Street
London W1R 6AH

Antique reproduction and contemporary lighting.

Lion Witch & Lampshade
89 Ebury Street
London SW1W 9QU

Lampshades made to order.

London Lighting Company
135 Fulham Road
London SW3 6RT

Modern lighting designs – Arteluce Artemide and Ingo Maurer. Mail order available.

Lloyd Davies
14 Dalton Street
Manchester M2 6JR

Modern architectural lighting from Europe. Repair service and design consultancy.

Louis Poulsen
MDS Services Ltd
Unit 9 Hewitts Industrial Estate
Elmbridge Road
Cranleigh, Surrey GU6 8LW

Distributor of Louis Poulsen lighting. Call for retail outlets.

Marlin Lighting Ltd
Handworth Trading Estate
Hampton Road, West Feltham
Middlesex TW13 6DR

Specialize in outdoor lighting.

Mathmos
179 Drury Lane
London WC2B 5QF

Witty 1950s-style lava lamps.

Maryse Boxer Designs
26 Sloane Street
London SW1X 7LQ

Stylish French lighting designs.

McCloud & Co
269 Wandsworth Bridge Road
London SW6 2TX

Traditional table lamps.

Mog Contemporary Lighting
127 Peperharow Road
Godalming, Surrey GU7 2PW

Contemporary lamps made from natural materials. Trade supplier call for retail outlets.

Mr Light
279 Kings Road
London SW3 5EW

Modern and traditional lights.

National Inspection Council for Electrical Installation Contracting
Vintage House
36–37 Albert Embankment
London SE1 7TL

Council to protect consumers against unsafe electrical installations. Contact for a list of approved contractors.

Nice House
Italian Centre Courtyard
Ingram Street
Glasgow G1 1HD

Modern styles including those of designer Mike Stoane and design studio Brainbox.

Ocean Home Shopping Ltd
9 Hardwicks Way
London SW18 4AW

Fun lighting and candle holders. Mail order catalogue.

Optelma Lighting
14 Napier Court
The Science Park, Abingdon
Oxfordshire OX14 3NB

Minimalist lighting systems. Trade supplier call for retailers.

Outdoor Lighting
3 Kingston Business Centre
Fullers Way South
Chessington, Surrey KT9 1DQ

Floodlighting, spotlights and underwater lighting systems.

Period Brass Lights
9A Thurloe Place
London SW7 2RZ

Restoration and cleaning of chandeliers. Also traditional brass desk and picture lights.

Porto Romana
West End Farm
Upper Froyle near Alton
Hampshire GU34 4JR

Makers of traditional and modern lights. Specialize in painted lamp bases.

Price's Patent Candle Co.
110 York Road
London SW11 3RU

Candles of all colours scents shapes and sizes.

Purves & Purves
80-81 Tottenham Court Road
London W1P 9HD

Contemporary lighting styles.

Reggiani Lighting Ltd
12 Chester Road
Borehamwood, Herts WD6 1LT

Manufacturers and importers of contemporary lighting. Trade supplier call for retailers.

Renwick & Clarke
190 Ebury Street
London SW1W 8UP

Wood, ceramic and metal floor, table and wall lights.

R Wilkinson & Son
1 Grafton Street
London W1X 3LB

Reproduction glass chandeliers and candelabras. Restoration, repair and cleaning service.

Ryness Electrical
45 Old Compton Street
London W1V 5PN
For branch details

A wide range of lighting essentials including switch plates and bulbs.

Selfridges
400 Oxford Street
London W1A 1AB

A wide range of lighting styles. Offer made-to-measure lighting schemes.

SKK
34 Lexington Street
London W1R 3HR

Innovative lighting in unusual materials. Architectural lighting consultancy.

Space
214 Westbourne Grove
London W11 2RH

Design classics of the future including one-off pieces.

Stiffkey Lampshop
Stiffkey
Norfolk NR23 1AJ.

Original antique lamps with glass shades dating from 1800 to 1930s. Reproductions can be commissioned.

Tindle Antiques and Decorative Lighting
162 & 168 Wandsworth Bridge Road, London SW6 2UQ

Original and reproduction lighting including chandeliers floor lamps and table lamps. Silk shades made to order.

TseTse at Galerie Sentou
26 Boulevard Raspail
75007 Paris, France

Stylish French lighting designs.

Vaughan Lighting
156–160 Wandsworth
Bridge Road
London SW6 2UH

Antique and reproduction light fittings. Trade supplier call for retail outlets.

Viaduct
1–10 Summers Street
London EC1R 5BD

Famous names in modern lighting (such as Ingo, Maurer, Flos, Arteluce and Pallucco).

Wandsworth Electrical Ltd
Albert Drive
Sheerwater
Woking, Surrey GU21 5SE

Decorative metal sockets and switch plates. Trade supplier call for retail outlets.

Wax Lyrical
61 Hampstead High Street
London NW1 1QH

For candles and candle-holders of all types and styles.

West Midland Lighting Centre
10–12 York Road
Erdington
Birmingham B23 6TE

State-of-the art lighting. Design service available.

William Yeoward
Space 5
The Old Imperial Laundry
71 Warriner Gardens
Prince of Wales Drive
London SW11 4XW

Metal light fitttings.

Wilchester County
The Stables, Vicarage Lane
Steeple Ashtom
Trowbridge
Wiltshire BA14 6HH

Metal chandeliers made to authentic 17th- and 18th-century American designs.

Wilkinson
5 Catford Hill
London SE6 4NU and
1 Grafton Street
London W1X 3LB

Reproduction chandeliers and restoration of glass chandeliers.

Woolpit Interiors
The Street, Woolpit
Bury St Edmunds
Suffolk IP30 9SA and
G13 Chelsea Harbour Design
Centre, London SW10 0XE

Traditional chandeliers and lamps. Shades made to order.

index

Page numbers in *italic* refer to illustrations and captions

a

accent lighting, 9, 14–16
  stairways, 15
alcoves, 15
  concealed lighting, 30
  hallways, 23–4, *23*
  living rooms, 30
ambient lighting, 9, 10–11
  bedrooms, 69–71, *69–71*
  kitchens, *10*, 44–5
  living rooms, 27
  studies, 84
Anglepoise lamps, studies,
  84

b

background illumination, 9
bare-wire installations, 6
  described, 30, 123, *123*
  dining rooms, 57–8,
    57–8
  kitchens, *44–5*
  living rooms, 31
  see also low-voltage
    halogen lighting
bathrooms, *88–101*, 89–101
  candles, 101, *101*
  colour, 92–3
  concealed sources, 97
  feeling of space, 98
  fluorescent lighting,
    93–4, 95, 97
  highlighting features, 101
  low–voltage halogen
    lighting, 99
  mirrors, 89, 94–6,*94–6*
  natural lighting, 90–1,
    90–1
  safety, 101
  texture, 92–3
  under–floor lighting,
    98–9, *98*
  wall lights, 99–100
bedrooms, *66–79*, 67–79
  adding atmosphere, 78
  ambient lighting, 69–71,
    69–71
  bedside lamps, 72–3,
    72–3
  dressing areas, 75–7
  flexible lighting, 73–4,
    73–4
  mirrors, 71, 76–7, 77
  natural light, *10*, 28, 68,
    68
  task lighting, 12, 13
  wardrobes, 77, *77*
blinds, *10*
  bathrooms, 91
bluish light, countering, 11
building, floodlighting, 106
bulbs:

crown silvered, 13
  halogen, 6
  types of, 115, 116–17,
    116–17

c

cabling, gardens, 103
candelabras, *58*
candles, 16, *17*
  bathrooms, 101, *101*
  bedrooms, 78, *78*
  dining rooms, 58–61, *65*
  gardens, 108
  hallways, 24
  kitchens, *43*
  living rooms, 35
central lights, 30–2
  see also pendant lights
chandeliers, 9, 16
  dining rooms, 58–60, *59, 60*
  living rooms, 32, *32*
children's rooms, 78–9, *79*
colour temperature, 115
colours:
  bathrooms, 92–3
  bedrooms, 68, 70–1
  daylight, 11
  decor, 30
  gardens, 104
concealed lighting, living
  rooms, 30
conservatory dining areas,
  56–7
contemporary styles, 6
cookers, 52
crown–silvered bulbs, 13
cupboards, kitchens, 51–2
curtains, living rooms, 28–9,
  28–9

d

daylight, 11
  bathrooms, 90–1, *90–1*
  bedrooms, 68, *68*
  conservative dining, 56
  dressing areas, 75, *76*
  gardens, 104
  hallways, 20–1
  kitchens, 43
  living rooms, 28–9
  studies, 82–3, *82–3*
daylight bulbs, 11
decorative lighting, 16–17
  hallways, 24
  living rooms, 35
dichroic reflectors, 6
diffuse lighting, ambient
  lighting, 10–11
dimmer switches:
  bedrooms, 73
  dining rooms, 56
  dressing areas, 76
  kitchens, 47
dining rooms, 54–65
  candles, 58–60, *58, 65*

centrepieces, 61
  chandeliers, 58–61, *58, 60*
  conservatories, 56–7
  dimmer switches, 56
  display units, 64, *64*
  outside, 107–8, *108*
  parties, 64–5, *65*
  pendants lights, *60–1*,
    61–3
  table lamps, *62–3*, 63–4
displays:
  dining rooms, 64, *64*
  hallways, *14*, *15*
  living rooms, 34, *34*
doors, hallways, 20, *20*
downlighters:
  accent lighting, 15
  alcoves, 15
  described, 119–20, *119*
  dining rooms, 57–8
  dressing areas, 76
  kitchens, 45–6, *45*, 50
  task lighting, 12
drapes, 28–9, *28–9*

e

eating areas:
  dining rooms, 54–65
  kitchens, 50–1
  outside, 107–8, *108*
entrances, 104–6, *105*
  see also hallways
exterior lighting, *102–13*,
  103–13
  entrances, 104–6, *105*
  floodlighting buildings,
    106
  lighting plants, 109–11
  pathways, 106–7, *106–7*
  patios, 107–8
  quality of light, 104
  roof gardens, 111–12, *111*
  safety, 103, 113
  statues, 112, *112*
  water features, 113, *113*
eyeball spots, 30

f

fairy lights, 16
fan lights, 20
fibre–optic lamps, 9, 17
firelight, 35
floor–standing lights, *31*
  bedrooms, 76
  described, 118–19, *119*
  living rooms, 36
  studies, 87, *87*
floors:
  accenting materials, 15
  under–floor lighting,
    98–9, *98*
flowers, downlighters on,
  23, 24
fluorescent lighting:
  advances, 6
  ambient lighting, 10

bathrooms, 93–4, 95, 97
  bulbs, 116, *116*, 117
  kitchens, 42–3, 44–5
  stairways, 25, *25*
fountains, 113, *113*
French windows, 20, 28
fun lighting, 16
furniture, living rooms, 30

g

gardens, *102–13*, 103–13
  entrances, 104–6, *105*
  floodlighting buildings,
    106
  lighting plants, 109–11
  pathways, 106–7, *106–7*
  patios, 107–8
  quality of light, 104
  roof gardens, 111–12, *111*
  safety, 103, 113
  statues, 112, *112*
  water features, 113, *113*
glare, task lighting, 12, 13
glass bricks, *7*
  bathrooms, 91, *91*, 100,
    100
glass displays, accenting, 14,
  15, 34, *34*
glazed doors, 20, *20*

h

hallways, *18–25*, 19–25
  alcoves, 23–4, *23*
  candles, 24
  decorative lighting, 24
  natural light, 20–1
  switches, 23
  table lamps, 21, *21*
  theatrical effects, 23–4
halogen lighting, 6, 117
  see also low voltage
    halogen lighting
highlighting features, 14–15
hobs, lighting, 52, *52*
horizontal illumination, 14

i

intimate atmospheres, *11*

k

kinetic lighting, 9, 16
kitchens, *40–53*, 41–53
  ambient light, *10*, 44–5
  cookers, 52
  cupboards, 51–2
  downlighters, 45–6, *45*,
    50
  eating areas, 50–1
  fixed lighting, 45
  fluorescent lighting,
    42–3, 44–5
  hobs, 52, *52*

integral fittings, 53
layouts, 42
natural light, 43
safety, 53
task lighting, 12, *12*
work surfaces, 50

l

landings, 19, 25
lava lamps, 9, 16, *17*
light:
  colour temperature, 115
  sources of, 115
living rooms, 27–39, *28–39*
  ambient lighting, 27
  curtains, 28–9, *28–9*
  displays, 34
  flexible lighting, 36
  floor lamps, 37
  furniture positions, 30
  intimate atmospheres, *11*
  light fittings, 30
  multiple light sources,
    30, *32*
  natural lighting, 28–9
  pendant lighting, 30–2
  reading lights, 37
  soft furnishings, 30
  table lamps, 36–7, *36–8*
  task lighting, 12, *13*
low–voltage halogen lighting,
  6
  accent lighting, 14, *14*
  bathrooms, 99
  bedrooms, 69, 73–4
  bulbs, 117
  chandeliers, 32, *32*, 60,
    61
  daylight effects, 11
  dining rooms, 57–8, *57–8*
  display lighting, 23, 34
  kitchens, 44, *44–5*, 47–50
  living rooms, 30, *31*
  studies, 86–7

m

mirrors:
  bathrooms, 89, 94–6, *94–6*
  bedrooms, 71, 76–7, *77*
  conservatories, 56
  hallways, *20*, 21
mood, 6
movable lighting, task
  lighting, 12–13
moving lighting, 9, 16

n

natural light, 11
  bathrooms, 90–1, *90–1*
  bedrooms, 68, *68*
  conservative dining, 56
  dressing areas, 75, *76*
  gardens, 104
  hallways, 20–1

kitchens, 43
living rooms, 28–9
studies, 82–3, *82–3*
neon signs, 9, 17

o

opaque shades, 13

p

parties:
  dining rooms, 64–5, *65*
  hallway candles, 24
pathways, 106–7, *106–7*
patios, 107–8
pendant lighting:
  advances, 6
  ambient lighting, 10
  bathrooms, 93, *93*
  described, 120–2, *121*
  dining rooms, *60–1*, 61–3
  dressing areas, 75
  hallways, 21–3, *21*
  kitchens, *42*
  living rooms, 30–2
  studies, 84, *84*
pictures:
  hallways, *22–3*, 23
  living rooms, 39, *39*
plants, lighting, 109–11
porches, 104–6, *105*

r

reading lights, 37
roof gardens, 111–12, *111*

s

safety:
  bare–wire installations,
    6, 49
  bathrooms, 101
  candles, 24
  gardens, 103, 113
  kitchens, 53
  low–voltage halogen
    lighting, 6, 49
sconces, 78
shades:
  bedside lamps, 72–3, *72–3*
  opaque, 13
  pendant lights, *60–1*,
    61–3
  table lamps, 118, *118*
shrubs, lighting, 111
shutters, windows, *10*
sitting rooms, 27–39, *28–39*
  ambient lighting, 27
  curtains, 28–9, *28–9*
  displays, 34
  flexible lighting, 36
  floor lamps, 37
  furniture positions, 30
  intimate atmospheres, *11*

light fittings, 30
multiple light sources,
  30, *32*
natural lighting, 28–9
pendant lighting, 30–2
reading lights, *31*
soft furnishings, 30
table lamps, 36–7, *36–8*
task lighting, 12, *13*
skylights, 43
soft furnishings, living
  rooms, 30
space, creating, 35
spotlights:
  accent lighting, 14–15
  described, 120–1, *121*
stairways, 19
  highlighting, 15
  lighting, *22*, 24–5, *24–5*
  pictures, *22*
standard (floor–standing)
  lamps, *31*
  bedrooms, 76
  described, 118–19, *119*
  living rooms, 36
  studies, 87, *87*
statues, garden, 112, *112*
studies, *80–7*, 81–7
  ambient light, 84
  decorative lighting, 87,
    87
  floor–standing lights, 87,
    87
  halogen lights, 86–7
  natural light, 82–3, *82–3*
  pendant lights, 84, *85*
  task lighting, 84–7, *84–7*
switches, hallways, 23
  see also dimmer switches

t

table lamps:
  bedside lamps, 72–3, *72–3*
  described, 118
  dining rooms, *62–3*, 63–4
  hallways, 21, *21*
  living rooms, 36–7, *36–8*
task lighting, 9, 12–13
  bedrooms, *12*, 13
  bedside lighting, 72–4
  described, 122, *122*
  kitchens, 12, *12*
  sitting rooms, 12, *13*
  studies, 84–7, *84–7*
television, lighting for
  watching, *38*, 39
terraces, 107–8
texture, bathrooms, 92–3
theatrical effects, hallways,
  23–4
torches, *108*
track lights, described, 123,
  123
trees, lighting, *109*, 111, *111*
tungsten lighting, 6
  bathrooms, 93, 99
  bulbs, 116, *116*, 117
  gardens, 104

intimate atmospheres, *11*
kitchens, 47–50
light from, 115
studies, 86–7
tungsten–halogen bulbs, 117
  see also halogen lighting
Turkish–style lanterns, 21,
  21, 32, 93

u

under–floor lighting,
  bathrooms, 98–9, *98*
uplighters:
  accent lighting, 14
  described, 120, *120*

v

Venetian blinds, *10*
  bathrooms, 90

w

wall lights
  bathrooms, 99–101
  bedrooms, 75–7
wall sconces, 78
wall washers, living rooms,
  30
wardrobes, lighting, 77, *77*
water features, gardens,
  113, *113*
windows, *10*, 11
  bathrooms, 90–1
  bedrooms, 68, *68*
  hallways, 20
  kitchens, 43, *43*
  living rooms, 28–9, *28–9*
  studies, 82–3, *82*
work rooms, *80–7*, 81–7
  ambient light, 84
  decorative lighting, 87,
    87
  floor–standing lights, 87,
    87
  halogen lights, 86–7
  natural light, 82–3, *82–3*
  pendant lights, 84, *85*
  task lighting, 84–7, *84–7*

acknowledgments

The publishers would like to thank the following sources for their permission to reproduce the photographs in this book.

Key
R: Right, L: Left, T: Top, TR: Top Right, TL: Top Left, C: Centre, CR: Centre Right, CL: Centre Left, B: Bottom, BR: Bottom Right BL: Bottom Left

Abode 10TL, 75T

Arcaid *Richard Bryant* 83; *Earl Carter/Belle* 33, 36R, 78R, 93TR, 95L, 95R; *David Churchill* 16, 51B; *Jeremy Cockayne* 63L; *Dennis Gilbert* 34T; *Nicholas Kane* 15B, 44, 98L; *John Edward Linden* 74L; John Edward Linden/Julian Powell Truck 10TR; *Trevor Mein/Belle* 10CR; *Paul Rafferty* 8; *Willem Rethmeier/Belle* 4CCL, 26, 39L, 63R; *Rodney Weidland/Belle* 68R; *Alan Weintraub* 15TL, 57R

Nikolei von Dimmlich 87B

Garden Picture Library *Michael Howes* 110; *Roger Hyam* 112; *Nigel Temple* 111L; *Ron Sutherland* 109

Robert Harding Picture Library/IPC *Jan Baldwin·97; Jennifer Beeston* 65T; *Dominic Blackmore* 21L, 76; *A Cameron* 20L, 108B; *S Dalton* 28L; *Andreas von Einsiedel* 90R; *David Giles* 72R; *Tim Goffe* 42; *Mike Greenwood* 93B; *Syriol Jones* 71; *Tom Leighton* 57L; *Nadia McKenzie* 32TL; *John Mason* 31TR, 31BR; *Marianne Materus* 12L, *Robin Matthews* 43B; *James Merrell* 31TL, 48, 52B; *Jonathon Pilkington* 17TL, 75B, 91B; *Nick Pop* 60R; *Peter Rauter* 65B; *Bill Reavell* 5CR, 88; *Trevor Richards* 92; *Pia Tryde* 85T; *Jerry Tubby* 69; *Polly Wreford* 61L, 91T

Harpur Garden Library 104

The Interior Archive *Fritz von der Schulenberg* 4CR, 24L, 25CL, 40, 49, 74R, 82TR, 93TL, 96T

Clive Nichols Photography 113B; *Garden & Security Lighting* 106, 113T

Octopus Publishing Group Ltd 46TL, 53L, *Paul Forrester/Reed* 121TR; *Peter Myers* 12R, 21R, 46B, 82B, 85BR, 87T, 90L, 96B, 99L, 120B, 123CR; *Polly Wreford* 15TR, 51C, 70, 72L, 82TL

Paul Ryan/International Interiors 4CL, 18L, 29TL, 43TL, 56R, 59R, 84TL, 99R

Elizabeth Whiting & Associates 6, 20R, 22, 38, 43TR, 46R, 62, 86TL, 98R, 105, 107, 108T, 111R

With special thanks to the following companies:

Arteluce/Flos (Tel. 0171 258 0600) 85BL

Artemide (Tel. 0171 631 5200) 119T, 122TR

Chelsom Ltd (Tel. 01253 831400) 119B, 120T, 122L

John Cullen Lighting (Tel. 0171 371 5400) 5CR, 14, 23L, 25TL, 25TR, 34B, 52T, 64L, 64R, 100B, 102

Dorma (Tel. 0161 251 4468) 68L

Habitat (Tel. 0171 255 2545) 29TR, 35L, 37R, 60L, 73R, 86TR, 118L, 118R

Homebase (Tel. 0645 801 800) 32B, 45R, 53R, 86B, 114

Ideal Standard Ltd (Tel. 01482 346461) 100T

Ikea Ltd (Tel. 01604 708686) 1, 2, 4CCR, 5L, 5CL, 13, 17B, 28R, 29B, 31BL, 36L, 45L, 47, 50, 51T, 54, 56L, 58L, 66, 77TL, 77TR, 77B, 80, 84TR, 121TL, 123CR

Simon Keen Lighting (Tel. 01252 717818) 123T

Ligne Roset (Tel. 0845 6020267) 24R

Littlewoods Catalogue (Tel. 0800 600400) 17TR

Ocean Home Shopping (Tel. 0171 498 8844) 73L

Philips Lighting (Tel. 0181 665 6655) 11, 79

The Pier (Tel. 0171 814 5004) 35R, 37L, 78L, 101L

Christopher Wray Lighting (Tel. 0171 736 8434) 32TR, 58R, 61R, 116TL, 116TC, 116TR, 116B, 117C, 123CR